*IN RETREAT WITH THE SACRED
HEART*

IN RETREAT

WITH

THE SACRED HEART

By Francois Charmot, S.J.

TRANSLATED BY SISTER MARIA CONSTANCE
Sister of Charity of Halifax

NP

THE NEWMAN PRESS
WESTMINSTER, MARYLAND
1956

Nihil Obstat: JAMES A. O'DONOHOE, J.C.D.
Diocesan Censor Deputatus

Imprimatur: ✝RICHARD J. CUSHING, D.D.
Archbishop of Boston

Date: September 16, 1955

Introduction

The topics treated in this book are intended not to be read but to be meditated, more or less slowly, according to the inspiration of the Holy Ghost. That is why we have written them somewhat in the manner of the psalms, under the form of verses, strophes, and even dialogue. Each verse—or each strophe—should be considered in silence and in wordless communing with Jesus Christ.

There is no other counsel to give to souls whom the Holy Ghost teaches to pray. The more they hold friendly converse with Jesus Christ in deep recollection, the more their prayer will be conformed to the desires of God and to their own spiritual needs.

Those who feel no movement of the Holy Ghost should first make an act of humility, and then invoke the Blessed Virgin and the Holy Ghost. They should place themselves in the presence of Jesus Crucified, and contemplate Him as did Mary His Mother, and Saint John the Evangelist. After having read one of these meditations slowly and entirely, they should consider each verse and each strophe, resting as long as possible in the spiritual savor, in the affections, and in the acts of the virtues which the Holy Ghost silently suggests to them.

No special pattern or method, nor particular arrangement need be sought in the succession of prayers. The Holy Ghost alone can suggest to the retreatant, or to his director, the choice of one meditation rather than another, according to his interior dispositions and his needs.

If the same ideas recur in different meditations, the retreatant will draw from them more substantial fruit for his soul. Prayer is not a study. The mind which studies seeks the progress of thought; the soul that prays seeks to contemplate the object, to hold to it, to be transformed to its image by love, and as much as possible, to be united to God in charity.

The colloquy will be made with Jesus Christ on the cross. We represent Jesus to ourselves as He is seen in the Gospel, His side pierced by the lance, and we follow the interpretation of St. John, of the exegetes, and of the Fathers.

These prayers may accompany a preached retreat, or a retreat read from a book, to afford the retreatant a greater spirit of devotion and generosity.

FR. CHARMOT, S.J.

Contents

*IN RETREAT WITH THE SACRED
HEART*

I.   The Love of the Father

In an embrace of infinite tenderness
the Father in heaven and His eternal Son
lived ineffably happy.
The Holy Ghost, Their equal, proceeded
from Their mutual love.

The exchanges between the Father and the Son—
which we in our ineffectual language call
kiss, Word, or Gift—
were so delectable
that no human being could have the slightest conception of
    them.
But of these inexpressible communings
Jesus, who alone had experienced them,
has left us a few human echoes.

The Father said: Thou art My beloved Son.
In Thee I am well pleased.

(3)

Nothing can give Me satisfaction except Thee.

Thou art the Only One.

Everything that comes from My Son gives Me infinite rejoicing.

Whoever resembles Thee excites My interest,

whoever does not bear some trace of Thy countenance

is nothing to Me; he is as if he did not exist.

Thou art all My thought, all My utterance,

all My knowledge, all My wisdom, all My beauty.

Thou art the unspotted mirror of My splendor.

My magnificence and My glory I see in Thee

Thou art the life of My life.

It is only in loving Thee that My being is perfect.

But in Myself I find a strange stirring of love:

man, whom We have created to Our likeness,

has troubled My mercy in offending Us.

Once more the inebriation of Paternity has taken possession
    of Me.

This love which binds Us to each other

and which forms Our beatitude,

I wish to disclose to sinful man

by a sensible manifestation of Our love

so that the sinner, seeing it, touching it,

receiving it into his flesh

may also, in spite of his sin, become My son,

and so that My Paternity will be spread

over a multitude of children made to Thy image.
Then, in them, My merciful love
will rest content
seeing Thee in them and them in Thee.

What then shall We do in Our love for poor sinners
to manifest Our glory?
I will give to Thee, to Thee My Son, who loves Me infinitely,
a human heart,
a heart into which We shall pour Our own love,
a humanity in which Thy person will become incarnate with
    Our love,
a mouth which will speak to men of Our love,
hands which will accomplish the works of Our love,
pure blood which Thou wilt shed in testimony of Our love.
And all they who thirst for Our love
will be bathed in Our Holy Spirit.

When men learn that God, for the purpose of loving them
has a Heart so great, so generous, so disinterested,
so inflamed, so merciful,
when they see that this Heart is a burning furnace
of charity and of infinite compassion,
that it holds more love than the sun contains fire,
that this Heart has loved them so much that it has finally
    burst with love,

and that, pierced with a lance by My order,
it has remained eternally open
to give them access to Our beatitude,
then, perhaps, they will comprehend what is the length
and the breadth and the heighth and the depth
of the love of the Father, of the Son, and of the Holy Ghost.
Many souls will love Us somewhat as Thou lovest Me.
They will be associated in the ineffable spiration of the Holy
    Ghost.
That is all that I wish in My love:
to show what a Father and what a Son We are.

The Son, being the Word of God, was in perfect agreement.
His love responded completely to that of the Father,
His will to the will of His Father.
In the Trinity, He pronounced the FIAT of the Incarnation,
whilst Mary was to pronounce it upon earth.

My soul, do you comprehend why Jesus shows you His Heart?

II.   My Masterpiece

says the Father is the Heart of Jesus

My heavenly Father has told me: My masterpiece, My glory,
    is the Heart of Jesus.

O Father, whose love is ineffable,
thy words concerning the Heart of Jesus reveal to me
a sublimity which I did not conceive.
Now I understand that Thou dost establish Thy glory
in receiving homage from the Heart of Thy well-beloved Son,
for the love with which He loves Thee is alone worthy of Thee.
It is the love of Thy Son; it has infinite value.
And all that this love gives Thee and has given Thee
is the gift of God to God Himself.
This is something that the human heart could never attempt—
only the Heart of Jesus makes God a gift of God.

O Father, whose entire works are marvelous,
that Heart is the most wonderful of all Thy gifts.

Thou hast created the immaculate heart of Mary,
    Queen of Angels.
She was the most beautiful of creatures,
but she was not Thy masterpiece.
Infinitely superior to her, Thou didst create the Heart of Thy
    Son,
Thy Son, equal to Thyself—Thou didst create the love of the
    Incarnate Word.
Nothing more beautiful than this masterpiece
can be imagined.

And it is this masterpiece that Thou hast placed at our disposal,
that we may procure Thy greater glory.
Thanks to Thy bounty, my wealth exceeds in value
the riches of all creation.
If I offer the loving death of Jesus,
I glorify Thee immeasurably.
And that is true also of each beating of His Heart.
If I offer His prayers, His sufferings, His words,
His merits, His works, His watchings, and His sleep,
His innumerable acts of charity,
even those He performed as a tiny Babe—
any one at any moment of His life,
the least as well as the greatest,
from the crib to the cross,
O Father, I procure Thy greater glory

because, in union with Jesus,
I offer to the Father His Son, equal to Him
in substance and in love.

What a great blessing, O infinitely good Father,
to be permitted to glorify Thee,
by offering Thee the love of Jesus Christ
in a new oblation,
which is that of God!
Yet here I have an unlimited succession
of oblations of equal value
to Thy greater glory,
made possible for me through the Heart of Jesus.

For Thou hast willed that Thy Son, the sovereign Priest,
should renew at each minute of the day
with the same love as in the Cenacle and on Calvary,
the oblation of a real sacrifice,
that of His immolated body and of His poured-out blood.
This sacrifice, kindest of Fathers, I can offer to Thee at every
    instant,
for Thy greater glory.

For the love of the Heart of Jesus,
ever glowing, as in the Cenacle and on the Cross,
directing toward heaven its immortal flames,

still offers Thee this eternal sacrifice,

from my lips and through my hands

and from my heart in which His Holy Spirit prays.

So it is, that in return for Thy love

and in the name of all those who are not aware of Thy love
　　for them

I can daily offer to God

the love of God,

to the Father the love of His Son.

But as time goes on,

just as the sun breaks through the buds in springtime,

the love of Jesus plants divine life in souls

and gives growth to what He has already sown.

Father of my Saviour, since the acts of love from Thy Son

exceed the graces granted at every hour,

it is not ten, nor a hundred, nor a thousand,

but an incalculable multiplicity

of new acts of love

that I can offer Thee each morning

in union with the Heart of Thy well-beloved Son.

They are infinitely agreeable to Thee,

because through me it is the Heart of God

who offers them to you—the Heart

of Thy Son who alone loves Thee

with a love equal to Thy fatherly loving-kindness.

What wealth, what power, what magnificence,
what divine splendor,
thou hast placed in my hands, O most loving Father!
Thy marvelous works are innumerable.
No man can be compared to Thee
in Thy benevolent designs toward us.
If I should attempt to relate them, I would find
them too many, far too many, for me to enumerate.
Oh my soul, bless thou the Lord
and never forget His benefits!

III.   Offer Me the Heart of Jesus

My poor children, said the Father of Jesus to sinful men,
you know I love you infinitely.
But you are so wretched and so miserable
in your nothingness and your sin
that I comprehend your despair of love.
When you try to show Me your gratitude
and to offer Me an agreeable sacrifice,
you succeed only in appearing
before so good a Father
like ungrateful and shamefaced children
who dare not lift their eyes toward Him.

With a generosity which is part of My glory,
I have given you My only-begotten Son,
with such generosity that it might seem
that I love Him less than I loved you.
I have delivered Him to death that you may have life.
You will be eternally astonished by such love.

This Son, who is God Himself, has preferred the condition
   of slave
to that of God among you.
He has redeemed you by His blood,
He has given His flesh for you to eat
in order that you might form but one body with Him.
Our benefactions are vast and innumerable.

But what can We expect from you in return?
From you, dependent creatures, who possess nothing of your
   own,
nothing but a will growing ever weaker,
ever more sinful, ever more indebted.
Ah, I understand how Our measureless generosity
could give birth in your heart to a despair of love
growing deeper every day!

This despair has wounded
my Son and Me and Our Holy Spirit
more than did your wretchedness, more than did your sin.
If by our generosity we succeeded only
in creating such an abyss of separation,
our love would have been terribly deceived.

But have you thought of the masterpiece of Our infinite wisdom? Of the Heart of Jesus?

(13)

Do you know that in Him and through Him you have
all the riches that can supply your deep wants?
Is not His love, which has inflamed His merits,
your good, *your* treasure, *your* heritage, *your* power?
Do you believe that the Word has been enriched by His
   Incarnation?
Do you believe that He had greater happiness on earth than
   He already possessed eternally?
No! Neither He nor I would have gained anything by associating ourselves
with your sinful and sorrow-laden flesh,
if man did not gain a love worthy of God
and for the glory of God.

It is man who alone has gained, gained everything.
Such is the law of Our love.
The Heart of Jesus has been created to enrich man
with His infinite merits and with His measureless love.
Consider then the immense glory
which you can offer Us by your filial love,
giving to the Father the love of God in Christ
and in the Holy Spirit.
What a blessing for you to reach, through My incarnate Son,
to equality of love with God.
He makes you a sharer through grace in the Spiration of the
   Spirit of Christ,

then He places in your hands His divine Heart,
His divine flesh, His divine blood, His divine merits
in order that by offering Him, you may give
the Father the same Gift as does the Son—
and all this in the faith and the charity
which the Holy Spirit infuses into your souls.

There is no further possibility of despair when you have the
    Heart of Christ.
Then offer to your Father this Heart which is infinitely pleas-
    ing to Him.
Then offer to your Father the prayers of the Son when you
    pray,
His merits when you work
His love when you love
His sacrifice when you sacrifice self,
and His death when you die.
Then you will have given the Father all that He expected
    from you
when He showed you such deep tender care.

IV. Filial Abandonment to the Father

If I did not not have some knowledge of the Heart of Jesus,
how little would I realize the love of our Father!
But, looking upon the pierced Heart of the Incarnate Word,
I can say with assurance:
blessed be Thou, O Father of Our Lord Jesus Christ,
who, in Him, has heaped upon us
all Thy spiritual blessings!
Before the creation of the world Thou hast chosen us in Jesus,
in order that we may be holy with Him
Through the love of the blessed Trinity.

Thy Son is charity, as Thou, Father, art charity.
He is all charity, as Thou art all charity.
The charity of the Father, of the Son, and of the Holy Ghost
is the same, equal in Three Persons.
There are not three charities, but one single coeternal love.
With what love I have been loved infinitely
neither more nor less by Thee, Father, than by Thy Son and
    by Thy Holy Spirit,
since before the creation of the world!

If I believe that Jesus loves me, I believe that His Father loves
     me just as much,
and when Jesus says to me that He will come to dwell in me,
it is Thy Word who declares to me that Thou, Father,
and Thy Holy Spirit wish to dwell in me.
All those whom the Heart of Jesus loved:
His disciples, the children, the sinners, the diseased,
the poor, the humble, the persecuted,
Thou, Father, also loved them with the same love.
The Blessed Virgin was loved no less by Thee
than by Thy Son, her Son, and by Thy Spirit.

O Father of Our Lord Jesus Christ,
blessed be Thou for having foreordained that we
should be Thy sons in Thine only begotten Son,
sons of adoption through Thy Son incarnate.
Thou hast willed, by this gracious predestination,
that the Heart of Thy well-beloved Son
should make us sharers in the love
of the Father, of the Son, and of the Holy Ghost.
For this Heart encompasses all that the charity of the Three
     Persons
could communicate from its Fire to the Incarnate Word.

In this Heart we possess by heritage
such an effusion of the Holy Spirit, such a furnace of love,
such an ocean of mercy,

such an outpouring of tenderness,

that it is impossible to imagine any others

in some perfect creature

which would be closer to infinite charity.

That is why, O Father, we know Thy love

through the Heart of Jesus.

Kind Father, kindest of Fathers, incomparably kind Father,

Thou hast willed that through the pierced Heart of Thy Son,

we should know the extent of Thy charity,

Thy goodness, Thy paternity, Thy longanimity,

Thy mercy, Thy pardon, Thine eternal remission of sin.

And when this Heart which has so loved men—

even to the shedding of all Its blood for them—

finally ceased to beat,

the death of Thy Son bore witness,

even as the sacrifice of His Father who had delivered Him,

that the love of the Three Persons for us

outweighs the very life of the Man-God.

Through the pierced Heart of Thy Son, O infinitely good

Father, grant me the grace to believe implicitly in Thy love,

to love Thee as a Son, as Thy Son Jesus,

who abandoned Himself to Thee in the agony and on the cross

in utter helplessness and total destitution,

solely because Thou wert His Father.

I cast myself into Thy paternal arms, as a prodigal son,
knowing that Thou art more kind even than my Mother Mary,
more loving even than the Heart of Jesus,
through whom I have come to know the immensity of Thy love.

Pater, in manus tuas commendo spiritum meum.
Father, in life and in death, in dangers,
in temptation, in sin, in doubt,
in error, in the folly of my heart,
in grief, in discouragement,
everywhere and always, whatever may happen,
united with the Heart of Jesus, I abandon myself
to Thy paternal goodness, source of all goodness.

V. Our Father

Our Father, who art in heaven,
Father of Jesus, and my Father,

hallowed be Thy name
through the Heart of Jesus,
whose filial love and merits I offer Thee!

Thy kingdom come
through the Heart of Jesus
whose blood, shed for us, I offer Thee,
and the wounds still open.

Thy will be done
through the Heart of Jesus,
whose "Ita Pater" I recall to Thee, oft-repeated by Him
even to the death of the cross
and to the final consummation
of Thy eternal designs.

Give us this day our daily bread,
and especially our true daily bread,
the flesh and the blood of Jesus,
which Thou didst give to Thy dear Son
through the immaculate Virgin
for love of us.
He Himself, in His love, gives them to us
that our hearts may be like His
and that we may share in His divinity
through the power of His Resurrection.

Forgive us our trespasses
through the Heart of Jesus who has already pardoned them
and who has washed them in His blood.
Through that Heart, always open to sinners,
through that Heart, the sure hope of all penitents.
It is Thou, our Father, who hast given us
this Heart which Thou didst will to be pierced
as pledge of Thy infinite mercy
and to stay Thy justice in advance.
Through it all love's refugees are saved.
Forgive us our trespasses

as we forgive those who trespass against us
in imitation of the Heart of Jesus
who abandoned the whole flock

(21)

to follow a single lost sheep
and who left His house, His work, His happiness
to bring home the prodigal child;
the Heart of Jesus who daily absolves
the Magdalen, the Samaritan, the adulterous woman,
the good thief, and even the privileged disciple
chosen, after his denial, to succeed Him;
this Heart which even to the end of the world purifies with
    its blood
every sinner whom every priest absolves
in the sacrament of His mercy.
O Father, if through Thy grace, the Heart of Jesus is in us,
we possess it in order that our hearts may, like His, pardon
without measure, seventy times seven times, the same enemies—
or friends—who wound them.
Ah! How pleasing to Thee is this resemblance.
This likeness—all those whom we pardon—
is the sure guarantee that Thou wilt pardon us.
O Jesus, make my heart like unto Thine.

And lead us not into temptation,
especially the temptation to doubt.
Grant that we may never doubt the Heart of Jesus,
His love, nor our love which comes to us from Thee.
For if we doubt the Heart of Jesus,
to whom shall we go, my God? Who would love us

as He has loved us?
In whom could we believe?

But deliver us from evil,
from evil and the wicked one, from Satan, Thy sole enemy,
from him who did not believe that the Father is love
nor that the Son and the Holy Ghost are love
and who, in consequence, has despaired for all eternity.
Father, Son, and Holy Ghost, through the Heart of Jesus
receive us into Thy love
into Thy holy and blessed Trinity.

Amen

VI. Mary Our Mother

Holy Mary, Mother of God, I firmly believe
that you are my Mother.
Jesus and His Church have expressly told me so—
but I am still more certain
that you are the Mother of Jesus.
It is through you that He became man.
You gave Him your blood and His blood,
your immaculate body and His divine body.
.All His humanity came forth from you,
through the power of the Holy Ghost,
as His divinity comes from the Father through generation.

When the Father willed to manifest His love sensibly,
He asked you to give to His Son
a Heart capable of containing and revealing His love.
You gave Him that Heart and you formed it,
a Heart so great, so pure, so generous,
that the love of God was revealed through it

as the sun is revealed through crystal—
just as it was in Himself.

That Heart whose fibers you formed,
whose feelings and inclinations you animated,
like every mother, you felt beating
under your fingers, against your cheek, on your heart.
Every vibration of that Heart
was that not of a man, but of a Man-God
and every one was an expression of divine love.

If a single word of Jesus could create the world,
calm the tempests, heal the sick,
plunge Magdalen into an ecstasy of love,
what must have been for you the blessed vision
of a Son who flawlessly radiated the beauty
and the power of the love of God!
What happiness was yours at all times, O Mary,
what ineffable happiness!
How could any creature have partaken of such happiness
without dying of an excess of love!

O Mother of the Seven Dolors, Jesus gave you on Calvary
children unworthy of you,
unworthy of being loved by you and of loving you.
If I offer you my whole heart

in unreserved consecration,
like a mother filled with pity
you will accept the oblation.
You cannot be to me aught but Mother of Mercy.

I know that you love me because of the Heart of Jesus.
You love me because He has loved me;
you love me in Him and with Him.
Had Jesus not loved me so much,
I would not be your cherished child,
your infirm child, but all the same, your child.

What should I give you, O my Mother,
in return for all your gifts—
for all those tender comforts
which mothers give to their little ones?
Oh! what shall I render you for so much loving care?
He has delivered to me a treasure which now belongs to me.
I am sure that it will give you ineffable pleasure.

It is the Heart of Jesus; it is His love,
His love as a child, His love as a youth,
His love as a man and a Man-God,
His love as crucified and as risen,
His love as priest and as victim,
His entire love in His union with you.

In return for your motherly favors,
I offer you this Heart, O Mary,
as if this Heart were mine.
Like a voice with which I sing and which swallows up my own,
my poor heart is a star eclipsed in the sun,
a sudden, quick blaze in a burning brasier.
I offer you His Heart; what consolation for your Child
that the Heart of Jesus loves you in us,
that I love you with Him, like Him, through Him!

No, I no longer want to love my Mother Mary
except with the Heart of her Son Jesus,
except as Mother of Jesus
as my Mother in Jesus.
My love is lost in the love of Jesus for Mary
and that of Mary for Jesus.

There is no other way to love you,
virgin immaculate and Mother of God,
than to put on the way in which Jesus Christ loves you.
All other loves are borrowed from men.
They are only the ardors of human nature.
But the only ardor which your motherhood inspires in me
is the flame of the Holy Spirit.
This flame comes from the Heart of Jesus.
It is the same fire—I believe it—whose burning

you, as Mother, have felt.

With Jesus, O Mary, a hundred times a day, I call on you—
Mother—

for the simplest things in life

as well as for the greatest in the kingdom of God.

My Mother, I love you with the Spirit with which your heart
cherishes me,

and as the Heart of Jesus, your Son, cherishes you.

We are both your children.

Amen

VII.   My Cloister is Thy Heart

I am cloistered, my Jesus, by Thee;
whether or not I am a religious, Jesus, Thou hast cloistered me.
My cloister is a dwelling of fire,
a furnace in which the burning souls
sing the *Benedicite Dominum.*
Into my cloister, no one can enter
unless he wishes to be consumed by an eternal conflagration.

O you who knock, lay aside all hope
save that of being the prey of the flames.
My cloister is the opposite pole to hell.

My cloister has a door,
a door always open,
a narrow door like the two lips of a wound.
This door is really a wound,
a wound always bleeding,
always fresh and always active.

Flowing forth from it is a flood of living water and pure blood,
torrents of grace and of mercy
which would submerge the ungrateful earth.
This door is hidden in the night.
It cannot be seen if the eyes of faith are missing.
Faith alone reveals it
and discloses the way which leads thither.
The opening is free and easy.
Oh! Marvel! in a blinding light
the illumined eyes see that it has the form
of a deadly lance.
And a voice cries to me from the darkness:
it is the eternal Father Himself who delivered His Son
to glorify the love of the Father and the Son
and to open to us the Heart of Jesus.

Since the Father has reopened this paradise,
the door has never been closed.
Very few people of the world, poor blind men, pass through.
But the dwellers of the furnace of love
wish never to come out.

All cloistered religious have sought holiness,
but not all have passed
through the wound in the Heart of Jesus.
They pray, work, obey, and serve,

held by the chains of vocation
but not always by the fire of love.

Those who are cloistered in Thy love, O Jesus, do the same
    things,
but in freedom of spirit and of body,
and in the beatitude of their union with God.
And what joy in their soul!
Circumdedisti me laetitia: Thou hast encompassed me,
O Jesus, with Thine own joy.
Whoever dwells in Thee, says the Apostle of Charity,
does not sin.

Whoever sins, has not seen it, nor known it.
Every fear has disappeared,
every trial is love's burning,
every effort is a gift of self,
through the power of the Holy Ghost.

The poor world, shut up in itself,
buried in its selfishness,
has only mockery, groaning rage
against people cloistered by love.
But it entirely ignores that one cloister,
ever wide open,
which is the Heart of Jesus.

It ignores all the bottomless riches of Christ

because it never dares enter into this abyss of love.

It does not possess faith; it is afraid of God.

O Jesus, my cloister will always be Thy Heart.

Grant that I may know no other;

grant that I may have no other bonds than the flames of love.

Grant that, plunged in the plenitude of Thy grace,

I may participate more and more in Thy intimate life,

and, by Thee and in Thee,

in the blessed and fruitful life of Thy Trinity.

Amen

VIII.   If We Did Not Have Thy Heart

If we did not have Thy Heart, O Jesus,
I would become mad with grief and despair,
despair for the world which would no longer have any meaning,
despair for those who would wish to love Thee
and could not.
despair for those who sin and would doubt about their
   forgiveness,
despair for those who thirst and would have no living water,
despair for those who suffer and would feel abandoned,
   without anyone and without Thy Heart,
ah! if I did not have Thy Heart,
I think I would die of sorrow and agony.

People may say to me: You have God, your Father.
But without Christ Jesus, how would I know Him?
And can I be sure?
It is Thou, the Son, who taught me "Our Father."
It is Thou, the Son, who art the proof of all things.

(33)

O Jesus, the Father loves me only in Thee and by Thee.
That alone is absolutely certain.
If we did not have Thy Heart, O Jesus,
my hands would be empty for God and for my neighbor.
I have nothing to offer the Father but Thy love;
nothing to give my neighbor but Thy love.

    Then?

Without Thy Heart, my poverty is equal to my helplessness
and my helplessness is worse than nothingness.

If I did not have Thy Heart, O Jesus,
what would I go to church to seek?
Something from the priests of Jesus? at baptism? at penance?
Even in the Eucharist, without Thy love, I would find nothing,
no victim offered, no flesh to eat, no blood to drink—

    without Thy pierced Heart.

But since Thou hast given me Thy Heart,
delivering to me Thy Spirit of Love,
I am carried away with gratitude,

    with joy and with trust. . . .

For in Him I possess
the fountain which quenches my thirst,
the fire which purifies my soul, inflames and consumes it,
the blood of sacrifice and of redemption,

the assurance of God's glory,

the salvation of souls,

a life of love in which it is no longer I who live

but Jesus Christ who lives in me.

Oh, Jesus, thanks, thanks, thanks,

thanks eternally.

IX.   What I Would Like To Be

Now and then, my God, Thou seemest to be asking me
how great a saint I would like to become
if Thou givest me sufficient grace.
This query makes me gasp . . . I, a saint?
I have not the courage even to think of it.

But Thou hast made me read the following story of
a child of fourteen years,
a little Russian, an orthodox, a foreigner:
enlightened by the Holy Ghost, he
found the answer that I sought in vain.
He was called Spiridon, and Thou hast made him
    Archimandrite.

He said to his director, a holy man: "You know
I ask nothing from God.
I do not even ask to be a saint,

to shine as the sun.
But I would like to love Him with my whole being
so that no one might love Him more than I.
I would like to forget everything,
forget my parents, my home, all the world,
forget myself also,
and be transformed into love for Him.
I would no longer be a man,
but be all love for Him.

"One day when I was in the meadow talking to God,
I almost died in that prayer.
My heart was bursting, sweat poured from me,
I prostrated myself on the earth,
and at that moment, I was no longer myself.
I was no longer anything but love ardent as fire.
There, that is the love that I would be."
Yet this pure and noble child
did not know the Heart of Jesus Christ.
Ah! if he had known the love of God through the Heart of
    Jesus,
what a flame would have darted forth from his entire being!
O Holy Spirit who hast enflamed this child,
I am deeply ashamed when I see myself in comparison with
    him,
knowing all that the Heart of Jesus Christ has revealed to me.

If this child had heard the beloved disciple
bear witness that the true God is love,
that the Trinity is Father, Son, and Holy Ghost,
and that the Father has delivered His Son to death for love
    of us,
and that His Son, for love of us, has poured out all His blood,
and that He gave up His spirit, dying naked on the cross,
and that this Spirit is the infinite Love of the Father and the
    Son,

If this child had seen the Heart of God-made-man
pierced by a lance in order to give birth to His one Spouse
in the water and the blood of His wounds of love,
if he had learned, through Christ and through this beloved
    Spouse,
that God is not only the love which gives itself
but the love which lives in us,
a love through which each of us in his soul can burn,
in and by the Spirit who is a consuming
and purifying fire in the center of our renewed being.

If this child had thought that by the Eucharist,
he could nourish himself with love,
eat love with the flesh of Christ,
drink love with His blood,
not only as one drinks water at its source

but by becoming one flesh with Him who is love,
by receiving, through the flesh of the Incarnate Word,
the creating Spirit which is fire,
living water, charity, and holy unction.

If Saint Monica had taught this child
that the violent longing of his heart
to be only burning love,
despoiled of everything which had not been given,
had not come from himself, but from the love of the Heart
    of Jesus,
can I doubt that this child, sustained by the Holy Spirit,
    would have become in reality what he wished to be!

Then, like Jesus, he would have loved all men,
friends and enemies, just and unjust, good and bad,
persecutors and calumniators;
he would have let himself be despoiled of everything, even
    life itself,
desiring only to give all,
asking no man for anything except to be the object of his love,
no longer seeking aught, but loving more and more.

For in order to be son of the heavenly Father,
son of the same Father as Jesus Christ,
like Him, similar to Him,

he had to become so by love.

The creature, no matter how elevated one imagines him, remains nothing.

But if he receives the love of the Heart of Jesus,

he can live of the love which is God Himself.

O Jesus, why hast Thou revealed this truth to me

and placed before my eyes the example of this Russian child,

if not because Thou dost hope that I also may wish to be,

through the flame from the Heart of Christ Jesus,

love as ardent as fire,

love alone and nothing else,

destitute of everything in my need of love,

love for all and in all,

like a fire which is only fire,

like the Holy Spirit which is only Spirit.

What I would like to be, O Jesus,

is a creature aflame in Thy Heart.

Amen

X. I Am the Way, the Truth, and the Life

The blessed revelation of Thy pierced Heart,
O Jesus, has driven all darkness from my spirit.
Final explanation of all Thy mysteries,
single key to Thy entire Gospel,
it illumines my faith with a peaceful glow.
Because Thou hast Thyself been the witness
and the visible manifestation of the love of God,
I know all, I understand all, I accept all!
All is perfected in Unity.

I see the beginning and the end of Thy acts,
their life, their substance, their harmony:
everything in them is love of God
and charity of the Heart of Jesus Christ.
Thy words have the depth of an ocean
whose surface alone I perceive.
When Thou sayest: I am the Way,
I am the Truth, I am the Life—

if Thou openest Thy Heart to me, I hear
something quite different from an abstract lesson.

What is the Truth? the Way? the Life?
Thou answerest: It is I—and I stand speechless.
God knows how madly I love truth,
and, perhaps more madly still, life,
and all the ways that lead to life.
But if *Thou* art the Truth, the Way, and the Life,
we no longer speak the same language.

For my ways of thinking are too human.
If Thou wert the teacher of all savants and scholars,
I could understand how you might be the Way.
But that Thou art really the Truth,
as if outside of Thee all is error,
and at the same time the Life
as if outside of Thee all is death,
and that Thou art at once the End and the Way
as if all contradiction
Resolves itself in Thee—
that is what troubles my mind
and does not draw my heart,
whilst I am drunk
with that truth and that life
which I find in this world.

Shall I, too, listen to Thy words
as a pharisee, a scribe, a philosopher?
Or shall I believe truly that all Thy words
are proofs of love,
of the confidences of the Bridegroom to His Bride?
Lord, I cannot understand Thee
unless I put the question to Thy Heart.
Thou art, O Jesus, the Way that the Father has traced
to reveal the charity of the Three Persons.

Thou art the Way on which Thou, the first to have passed,
didst descend from eternal royalty to the poverty of the crib,
thence to remount with the cross to the right hand of the
    Father,
freeing all the sons of God from slavery and from death.

Thou art not a Way made by the hands of men,
according to calculations of scientific reasoning,
but a road marked by the drops of blood
which Thou didst shed without number;
a humble way of sorrow, of death, and of resurrection,
which is the royal way of sublime love.

If Thou art at the same time the Truth and the Life,
the Truth and the Life of Which Thou dost speak
can be attained only through charity,

by Thy merits, in Thy footsteps, in the imitation of Thy virtues,
in loving Thee devoutly,
in eating Thy flesh all along the way,
in living by the Holy Spirit which unites us to Thee.

If God is love,
there is only one passage from us to Him.
There is only one Pasch
which leads to Him.
It is a Pasch of blood,
it is a Pasch of love.

O Jesus, it is on the cross, with Thy Heart pierced,
that Thou art completely the Way, the Truth, and the Life.

XI.   To the Priestly Heart of Jesus

O Jesus, my devotion to Thy Heart,
treasure of all perfection and of all mercy,
is inflamed with a new ardor
when I hear Thy Father proclaim
that Thou art Priest for all eternity.
Everything in Thee is priestly:
Thy human nature, Thy soul, and Thy body,
Thy lips, Thy hands, but especially Thy Heart.

Thy Heart, more than any of Thy members
is under the seal of the love of the Father and of the Holy
     Ghost.
For it is the love of the blessed Trinity which has united Thy
     two natures
by a divine unction, source of all unction.
It is love which spreads Thy unction
over all the priests of the Church
whom Thou hast consecrated to perpetuate Thy mediation.

It is love that has made of Thee a victim,

the sovereign Victim, alone agreeable to the Father,

the Victim of the crib, of the cross, of the altar,

the Victim of the whole Mystical Body, Thy eternal
holocaust.

Thy Heart is priestly in its every movement,

for all Thy work, O Jesus, is that of Thy priesthood,

and Thy priesthood itself is a priesthood of love.

How could I be unmindful of it when I contemplate Thy
Heart?

I exult with joy in calling Thy Heart priestly.

When I consider that Thy love is that of the eternal priest,

I seem to penetrate farther into its depths.

At first I see Thy Heart in the abyss of Thy humility,

for it has taken upon itself our lowliness and our infirmities;

I see it in the perpetuity of Thy oblation,

replacing and giving value to all other sacrifices.

I see it in Thy daily offerings to our Father.

One and the same Heart, in all tabernacles,

one and the same Heart, in all Masses,

one and the same Heart, in the celestial sacrifice

offered in this Tabernacle not built by men.

I see this Heart in the center of all liturgies,

praying through the voice of the faithful of all races,

inspiring the soul of the holy Church
when she speaks, sings, and weeps in the name of her Spouse,
in accord with the ten thousand saints marked with the
sign of the cross and of the blood of the Lamb.

I see it again in the members of all who are sick,
of all those who are persecuted, and all who are martyrs,
completing in their immolation
the redemption of sinful creatures,
mingling their blood with the blood shed by Christ
through the one same Holy Spirit.
And in everything and everywhere, I see Thy priestly Heart,
      O Jesus,
because the entire Redemption, love's labor,
is the triumph of Thy Heart and of Thy priesthood.

Stirred by this excess of love, O Jesus,
with what inexpressible fervor
I ask Thee to give me, miserable as I am,
a heart like Thine;
I mean a truly priestly heart.
It is my vocation, my ideal, my dream.
Can I presume even to love Thee,
or to love the Father or to love souls,
if I do not possess a priestly heart?
All other love seems alien to Thine,

too narrow, possessive, sterile,
if it is not like an unction of Thy priesthood.

A priestly heart like Thine,
O Jesus, is a heart consumed with love,
whose unquenchable flame mounts ceaselessly
to the infinite mercy of the Father,
ever more eager to glorify the Father
and to do His will even to the death of the cross,
a heart which is never tired of praying to the blessed Trinity
nor of offering to it all things human:
prayers, trials, works, and good deeds
in the plenitude of the sacrifice of Christ.

A heart which forgets self and immolates self
from the Mass of one day to that of the next,
to fill up what is wanting in the Passion of Jesus Christ,
a heart which gives, so to speak, all the blood of its veins
and spreads it everywhere
that souls may quench their thirst
by virtue of its daily oblation
of the very blood of Jesus Christ,
sovereign Priest and sovereign Host.

O Jesus, grant that the power and the sanctity of Thy
    priesthood

may possess my frail and guilty heart;
fill my heart with Thy holy oil,
consecrate it, consume it in Thy flame!
And grant that the Holy Ghost may spread abundantly
over all my members and over all my actions
the power of Thy holy sacrifice!

XII.   My Heart Like to Thine

O Jesus, who would dare pretend
to have a heart like Thine?
Thy Heart was formed from the immaculate blood
of the Virgin Mary, Queen of Angels;
Thy Heart was made for the greatest love
with which a creature could burn,
for the greatest sufferings and greatest goodness
that a man could ever experience.
Thy Heart was made not for a superman
but for a God-Man
according to the infinite mercy
of the Father, of the Son, and of the Holy Ghost.

There is no possible way of becoming equal
to such a Heart, whose perfection is limitless.
And yet the Church bids me pray thus:
Jesus, make my heart like unto Thine.
And the Son of God Himself, who knew His Father,

had already said: Be perfect

as your heavenly Father is perfect.

Is it a mockery? or does there exist a mysterious secret

for changing dross into pure gold?

The most chaste Virgin could listen to words

like those of the angel at the Annunciation,

and answer simply: "Be it done unto me according to Thy
word."

But the record of my heart takes birth in sin.

At baptism, the devil had to be driven out by the Holy Ghost.

Of itself, my heart is false, selfish, and hard,

so little capable of loving God and man

that our Lord has well named it a heart of stone.

But the Savior breathed upon it with His mouth

as on the day when God made man to His image.

And my heart, receiving the Holy Ghost,

began to be shaped according to the image of the Heart of
Jesus.

O blessed new creation!

O admirable reformation of my humanity!

Man can henceforth love as God,

by virtue of the Holy Ghost and of the charity infused into
him.

Water is changed into wine; wine, consecrated into the blood
of Christ.

Bread has become His flesh,

and behold my heart made like to the Heart of Jesus!

But how will my heart be able to love other than it has been
  loving?

The Church answers me: Through charity.

The charity of whom? The charity of Jesus Christ,

the charity which is a flame enkindled in His Heart

by the very spirit of Jesus Christ.

Through His Spirit, Jesus loved all men

but especially the unfortunate,

the poor, the meek, those who mourn,

those who hunger and thirst for justice,

the peacemakers,

those who suffer persecution for truth's sake,

those who are outraged and despised,

in short, all those for whom men have a natural repugnance.

Possessing the plenitude of Spirit, Jesus

loved also what the world abhors and repels:

privation, abandonment, destitution,

absolute sincerity, purity of soul and of body,

imprisonment, scourging, calumny, mockery,

Iniquitous judgments, the crown of thorns, the humiliating
  death,

sacrifice of self for the sake of another,
because to all the honors which were his due
He preferred the will of His well-beloved Father.

My child, when you pray in all confidence
for a heart like to that of Jesus,
you want to receive the Spirit of Jesus and His charity,
but, with these gifts, you do not want to receive
the love of all those creatures
that Jesus loved
but which your carnal heart cannot look upon without disgust,
nor accept without immediately rejecting them.

Ah! Jesus, how do our hearts—made to concur
in the love of all that is true,
beautiful, pure, great, and generous—
recoil when the Father asks
that we love His will in all things,
even those contrary to nature!
Thy Heart loves absolutely everything
with an infinitely pure love.
Mine does not like what is displeasing to it
even though it be pleasing to God.

Jesus, dare I hope that Thou wilt at length grant me
the grace of loving the chalice that Thy Father

has given me, and all those which He will give me?
The grace to take on myself the livery
which Thou wishest me to wear with Thee?
Jesus, meek and humble of Heart,
make my heart at length like unto Thine.

XIII.   The Answer from the Pierced Heart

Jesus, Thou hast just died on Thy cross.
With Thine eyes of flesh, Thou didst not see
the executioner break the legs of Thy companions.
With Thy dead ears, Thou didst not hear them
wondering if they should break Thy bones.
But the Word remained united to the inanimate body;
Thou didst see all, hear all, rule all, direct all.

At that moment, in order to fulfill the Scripture,
the Word sent the Spirit to the soldier who brandished the
    lance.
With a violent blow, he pierced the side of Jesus
and there came out blood and water.
What a response, O God of love, to the final crime of man
committed directly against the body of Christ,
even after His death; from the sacred wound
there began to flow an eternally prolific flood
of blood and of water, symbols of the sacraments.

All this brings me to the belief, O Jesus,
that God's way of acting toward us
has changed since Thy Heart was pierced.
This wound is the sign that the Old Testament was terminated
and that the New Testament has begun,
the Testament of the charity of Christ.

Up to the time of the opening of the Heart of Jesus,
great sins received an immediate recompense,
their just chastisement.
Adam and Eve disobeyed; they were driven from Paradise
and all their descendants were pressed down with misfortunes.
Cain killed his brother; he was struck with the sign of
    malediction.
Sin became universal; the deluge brought destruction
to sinners in like proportion.
Confusion of tongues dispersed the proud builders of Babel.
Egypt was submerged in catastrophes,
and all her first-born were put to death
because she held Israel in captivity.

Moses did not enter the promised land
because he did not immediately believe that his obedience
would bring forth from the rock the waters of Meriba.
What shall we say of the chastisement of Saul? of David?
Of Osee? And of so many other sinners?

(56)

They bore witness to the anger of God
against the proud who offend His infinite Majesty.

But what do I see here on the cross?
A God who is riddled with wounds and who pardons His
   assassins.
I see the Word of God select the hour of the final crime,
that of the blow from the lance, after a bloody death,
to give to men who are deicides and homicides,
to all mankind joined together in this base action,
an answer of universal and boundless love.

Out of this Heart, opened by a cruel blow,
the Word Incarnate brought forth the new Eve;
Holy Church filled with the Divine Spirit,
mother immaculate, like Mary, mother of all men,
source of divine light and of holiness,
pouring forth from her womb innumerable graces,
spouse of Christ, not only associated with Christ,
but engendered from the flesh and blood of Christ,
becoming by the Spirit of Christ adopted sons of God,
bringing forth through Him and with Him who is the Way,
   the Truth and the Life,
and giving brothers to the First-Born, Jesus Christ.
The blood and the water, flowing from His Heart signified
   this Mystery.

O Jesus, in this love, make my heart like to Thine.

In the turmoil of life, my sensitive and emotional heart

is often wounded by words and acts

which inflict upon me a piercing pain

like that of an open wound.

How does my poor ulcerous heart act then?

It returns evil for evil;

it takes immediate revenge, sometimes without reflection.

Often it closes up and grows hard

and walls up its own goodness till it grows embittered.

Each blow that is given me,

little or great, guilty or innocent,

just or unjust, hyprocritical or sincere,

should call forth from my heart

all the goodness which Jesus has placed in it;

the water, symbol of pardon, of mildness, of graciousness;

the water, symbol of candor and of simplicity;

the blood, symbol of the gift of self and of sacrifice;

the blood, symbol of generous and fruitful life.

O Jesus, through the infinite mercy of Thy pierced Heart

obtain for me the priceless grace of giving my life

drop by drop, for all those whom Thou hast redeemed

by Thy death and by Thy precious blood.

XIV.   Indifference Through Love

My child, Jesus Christ says to me,
you do not hesitate to say that in order to attain an end
you must take the means.
There is no other way to reach God,
to enjoy Him eternally,
than to do His will.
The creature does not make himself master of God as of any
    mere object.
God eludes all such domination.
God draws and leads to Himself
whom He wills, when He wills, and as He wills.

But such is His will,
that it is impossible to foresee the way
which He has traced for each of us.
Will it be a long or a short life?
Sickness or health? honors or humiliations?
authority or obedience? consolations or sufferings?

The way which leads to God is a daily hazard of faith
over unforeseen obstacles.
It is absolutely certain that you will go to God
only by the way which He Himself has chosen.

But there is always one thing
which He demands of you before all else,
always necessary, always inspired by the Holy Ghost.
It it to be ready for everything, disposed to do anything, no
    matter what,
no matter where, no matter how, according to the good
    pleasure of the Father,
so that you never prefer anything whatsoever
to the will of God.
Salvation, and even more, sanctity, is at this price.
Will you always, like Me
and like My Mother Mary, say: Yes?

Lord, I have nothing to say except that this perfection
is beyond my strength,
and that under such conditions, it would be useless
to make an attempt of fidelity.

My son, listen carefully to what I say.
God is a Father who holds His child by the hand,
a Father who can refuse nothing to prayer.

With His grace, the impossible is possible;
the difficult, easy; the harsh, sweet; the rigid, flexible.
The Ark of the Covenant divided the waters to make the
    Jordan passable,
the luminous cloud brightened the night for us,
the water spouted from the rock to quench thirst,
the manna gave us nourishment in the desert.
Have confidence; everything arrives at the end appointed.

Lord, in recalling the miracles of the Exodus,
Thou dost confirm my fears.
Neither I, nor anyone else, can count on miracles
to conduct us to our Promised Land.

My child, I have given you a thousand times more than
Moses with all his privileges.
I have given you My Heart, My pierced Heart.
For you, Moses is Jesus, the God of love.
The Ark of the Convenant is My Heart,
the luminous cloud, the open rock,
the living water and the manna and all the miracles
are only symbols of My pierced Heart
whence flow blood and water.

Take My Heart into your hands
as an offering to the Father

that He may illumine your way with His light.
Quench your thirst from the wound in the side!
Nourish yourself from the bread which I have consecrated,
and nothing will draw you more powerfully
than the holy will of God.

It is solely because My Heart
was the true Covenant, eternal, inviolable,
the light of light,
the source of pure and purifying water,
the true bread descended from heaven,
That, even in the most atrocious sufferings
it has never failed in one iota to do the will of the Father.
That is a wonder surpassing all miracles.

Now, my child, My Heart is with you, in you, and for you.
It is your prayer, your offering, your sacrifice,
your strength, your example, your companion,
your consolation, your victory, your thanksgiving.
It is your Ark of the Covenant
between your soul and God.
Have confidence, all that you expect from love
you will have a thousand times more from My Heart.

XV.   On Earth as in Heaven

Sanctity, My child, consists in doing My will.
There is no supernatural perfection imaginable
outside the accomplishment of My holy will;
for there is no perfection of which I am not the cause
by the gift of My Holy Spirit and of His grace.
Without Me you can do nothing, neither you nor anyone else.
I am the vine and you are only the branches.
The sacraments themselves do not produce their effects, un-
    less I will it.
Why do men lead an ascetical life and receive mystical graces?
It is to destroy every obstacle
to the union of their will with God's.
All the saints in heaven are there through My will.
They observed My commandments
and realized the designs which I had laid out for them.
The Blessed Virgin and Saint Joseph were perfect
by not omitting an iota of My will for them.

I Myself consummated the work of My Father,

doing only what was agreeable to Him, nourishing Myself
    with His good pleasure.

The perfection and happiness of the elect will consist eternally

in the unfaltering accomplishment of My will.

My will, always My will, nothing but My will.

You know that, My child. Why, then, are you so stubborn?

Is it not a monstrous error and folly

to prefer your will to Mine,

not to listen to My voice?

The number of the foolish is infinite,

Ah! Why are men deaf to My appeal?

—Lord, Thou knowest infinitely better than I,

men have a fear of Thee. They have no trust.

That is why they flee when they hear Thy voice.

They believe that Thou callest them to surrender all good
    things,

to imprison them, to enchain them, to condemn them

to wearisome work under an inhuman law.

If they knew the truth, if they believed in Thy love,

they would not run away, they would run to meet Thee,

they would eagerly enter Thy service.

Dare I say, My Lord and My God, that there is only one way

to captivate man to Thy will?

It is to make this law the law of love: *Voluptate trahitur.*

—My child, you are right: man has been created by Me
in such a way that he cannot resist love
for I am Love and unrivaled in love.
That is why I am all-powerful.
And, in order that man may love my will,
I have shown him My pierced Heart and I have said to him:
all My thoughts, My designs, all My laws, all My
    commandments
are dictated only by My Heart.
For such is the transcendent originality of My will
that it is always identical with My love.

If it were imposed only by My love,
man should receive it with an infinite gratitude;
but in Me will and love are one and the same thing,
more than light and heat are one in the sun.
It is because I love you that I will all that I will.
To obey Me is to yield to My love,
to observe My precepts is to be overwhelmed by My love.

My will is not, like that of men, an abstract rule.
It is the sign of the presence of the Spouse
when He desires to enter into your dwelling in order that you
    might enjoy His presence.
My "I will" signifies that I wish to live in your soul
and to unite Myself more intimately with it.

I have no other will than that of My Heart,
always the same, always loving, always beneficent.
If I did not love you, I would ask nothing of you;
if I loved you little, I would ask little.
When I ask much, it is because I love much.
You can always measure the ardor of My love
by the demands of My will.

—But, Jesus, My beloved Master, when men
wish to show their love,
their wishes are like beautiful ripe fruit
full of savor, of sweetness, and of delight.
Thy will is very often crucifying;
it seems to be a searing sword,
piercing, lacerating, agonizing.
And Thou sayest that it is dictated by Thy Heart. . . .

When we can no longer do our own will,
we pray thus: Lord, Thy will be done!
But as soon as we are free,
we prefer to act according to our own pleasure,
for our good pleasure is a glutton:
it gives us a relish for the joys of life.
Nothing is more intoxicating than liberty.
It deceives us into thinking that we are gods.
Thy good pleasure very often deprives us

(66)

of all that makes us laugh, sing, make merry.
Does Thy Heart know how much we love to be free?

—My child, what confusions cloud your understanding!
I Myself am the creator of liberty and I bring it to perfection.
I love liberty beyond all things.
I will never give you heaven under compulsion.
The happiness that I am preparing for you will be the fruit
    of your liberty.
You will enjoy it only in liberty and through your liberty.
My Holy Spirit is a spirit of liberty.
But true liberty abides in love. All others are false.
One is free to love or not to love the true life.
No matter what befell Me on earth,
my liberty, which was all-powerful, was in My Heart.
All My works, from My birth until My death,
I accomplished freely, because I did them through love.
In the crib, I was wrapped in swaddling clothes; on the cross,
    I was fastened by nails.
During My whole life, I was fettered to the will of My Father,
but I always acted freely because I always acted through love.

Men do not see that in following their passions
they are slaves of the creatures which seduce them.
The more they yield to their desires
the more they are powerless to do good.

They lose the liberty for the best things in life,
and sometimes even the most necessary.
In following their caprices, they lose the will
to be delivered from the enslavement of creatures.
My will must be done!

But My will is accomplished only through love;
it is love which renders men sovereignly free.
Your will united to Mine is all-powerful.
Fear, suffering and death do not paralyze it.
The martyrs were free to say no to the tyrants
because love is stronger than all sufferings.

If you wish true liberty, ask it of My pierced Heart.
Because it is the source of love, My Heart will give it to you.

—Ah! Jesus, I understand now:
the greatest act of love is to do Thy will.
The greatest act of liberty is to do Thy will.
Supreme wisdom, sovereign power,
absolute perfection, pure happiness,
the eternal fecundity of our human activity,
all good things are in the accomplishment of Thy will.
Poor, sick, humiliated, persecuted,
in misfortune as in prosperity,
whether my accomplishments are trivial or important,

provided that my will is united to Thine,
I am rich enough, I am godlike with Thee,
I live on earth as in heaven.

My God, I ask of Thee the grace of graces:
grant that I may never forget that Thy will is Thy love.
Thou dost command nothing except in love.
Thy law is that of Thy Heart.
Send forth to me the Spirit of the children of the Father
that I may in all things and at all times lovingly accomplish
the one holy will of the Three Persons
Father, Son, and Holy Ghost.

Amen

XVI.   Into Thy Hands I Commend My Spirit

If there is a death worthy of imitation, O Jesus, it is Thine,
not because it was filled with consolation, beautiful and
    triumphant,
but because it was that of God,
of the Christian God who is Love.
Infinite Love, in order to manifest itself to the world,
chose—in union with the Father—death.
Life chose death.
The Word chose the silence of death.
He who is the resurrection wished first of all to be brought
    to nought.

What a mystery! To a glorious death, O Jesus, Thou didst
    prefer
the shameful death of the cross.
When the priests had anathematized Thee,
when the heathen tribunals had condemned Thee,
when Thy own people in crowds had been false to Thee
when the executioners had led Thee like a sheep to the
    slaughter,

thou didst render Thy last sigh, and all was consummated.
That is what Thou didst choose through love.

Thy death, O Jesus, is the model for ours.
There are no other models; there is only one—Thine.
When I am asked: What kind of death do you want to have?
Oh! I do not hesitate an instant: It is that which most closely
    resembles
Thy death, O Jesus, Thy death on the cross.
Almost all deaths are borne on the cross,
but all crosses are not that of Jesus.
The bad thief rebelled against justice.
The good thief submitted through necessity,
yet he hoped for salvation from Jesus crucified.
Jesus, Himself, died because He willed to die,
in obedience to His Father, in testimony of His love,
in reparation for the crimes of His brethren,
to save them all through His Resurrection.
There is nothing more sublime than the death of Jesus.

Among the gifts that God makes to sinful man,
Jesus' death on the cross is the supreme benefaction.
Nothing, so much as His death, could exalt
the obedience and the love of man for God.
No other act is as reparative and redemptive
there is no other way to rise again
with Jesus to life eternal.

My God, why should I not love death,

source of so many graces for me and for souls?

I shall die but once. Will it be on the cross of Jesus?

Everything is unknown to me save the love of the Heart of
Jesus.

I am assured in advance that my death, like the whole story
of my life,

is inscribed in the Heart of Jesus.

His Heart has chosen for me the most favorable hour,

the gentlest and the most efficacious sufferings.

For a long time, His Heart has been preparing the graces

to make my death like unto His.

Ah! if my death, O Jesus, does not resemble Thine,

It is because the graces that Thy Heart has prepared for me

Have found my soul indocile to Thy love.

Yes, Jesus, I can fear all the circumstances of my death,

except that of being abandoned by Thee. That is impossible.

Thou hast a Heart a thousand times more tender than that
of a mother.

Thou wilt certainly be present to configure me to Thy death,

for it has always been the desire of Thy Heart

that I should expire with Thee, like Thee, and in Thee.

And to console me, to ease this terrifying passage,

Thy Heart has given me the maternal smile

of my sweet mother, the Virgin Mary,

who will be there at the foot of the cross of Jesus.

Henceforth, as her child, into her motherly hands
and into Thy hands, Jesus, I commend my spirit.
I wish to live this supreme hour in advance
so that it may be such as Thy Heart has desired,
that I may die on Thy cross, in Thy Heart.

May this death which Thou hast ordained for me,
by dying Thyself on the cross for love of us,
forever unite my will to that of our Father.
May it be my greatest act of love for Thee.
May it repair my faults and save souls.
May it open for me the narrow gate to paradise,
where I shall at length find Thee and possess Thee eternally,
with my soul living and purified, with my body restored to life,
for such a death is comformable to Thy Heart.

O Jesus, may Thy infinitely merciful Heart
grant me the grace to die as Thou willest,
to obey Thee, to love Thee without measure,
to participate in Thy redemption of mankind,
finally, to enjoy Thy presence
and the eternal vision of the blessed Trinity.

Amen

XVII.   Look upon Him Whom Thou Hast Pierced

Like the Good Thief and Magdalen, O Jesus, I contemplate
   Thee
crucified for love of me,
for me, a sinner, unworthy of raising my eyes to Thee.
If Thou wert to appear to me in the glory of Thy Resurrection,
filled with shame, I would lower my eyes because I am unclean.
There is only one image of Thee on which I can gaze,
because it is the work of my sins
and the truest expression of merciful love.
It is the image of Thy body covered with wounds
and of Thy pierced Heart whence stream forth blood and
   water.

Look upon Him whom thou hast pierced,
says the Holy Spirit to me in Scripture.
I see Him just as He is on the cross
More wretched than the slave described by Isaias.
He is such as I have made Him; for He is the victim of sin.

Sin consists not in disfiguring a man,

but in disfiguring a God.

The concentration camps and the battlefields

produced victims more atrociously mutilated

than the Servant of Yahweh,

but they were not the Word of God.

Jesus Christ alone is God. He whom we have transpierced

is none other than Jesus Christ, the only Son of God.

The gravity of sin comes from the fact that we have harmed

frightfully, God Himself, the only true God, Jesus.

O Jesus, send forth the light of Thy Holy Spirit

that I may at length understand the horror of my sins.

None of the misfortunes and the catastrophes of this world

are to be compared with sin; they are finite.

My sin offends not creatures, but God Himself.

This infinite offense against God seemed strange and incred-
ible to me,

both difficult to prove and difficult to believe,

when I reasoned about the divine nature, inaccessible as it is.

But the day came when God Himself died on the cross,

because my sins had wounded Him and put Him to death.

Ah! Then, it was impossible to hide my crime,

to seek excuses, to raise objections.

It is certain, my sin, whether I wish it or not,

has succeeded in doing what no power on earth could attempt:

the death of the Son of God, consubstantial with the Father,
for faith tells me that Jesus Christ died because of my sins.

No, no, it is not true; Jesus did not die
because men conquered and crucified Him.
He died freely because He willed it,
as He became incarnate of His own free will,
as, of His own free will, He delivered Himself to the
     executioners.
The sole reason for His death is sin.
Am I going to excuse myself by throwing the responsibility
on others and especially on great sinners?
One single wound, one single drop of blood
could wash all their crimes and an infinity of others.
But for a single one of *my* sins
one drop of blood was necessary.
Jesus shed His blood for me, a sinner, as for other sinners.
I have made the Son of God die: if this were not so, my faults
     would not be sins.

If some honorable judge would say to me: "You are a homicide,
you have murdered an innocent man; you have killed your
     best friend,"
I could swear that it is not true.
But if he said to me, "You have put to death the Man-God,
     Jesus Christ,"

I could not deny it—it is indisputable.
I would have to agree that it is true. Faith assures me that sin
is precisely what crucified the Son of God.

The chastisement of the rebellious angels,
the misfortunes caused by the disobedience of Adam
are fearful effects of sin.
But the measure of sin is not of human order;
it is of divine magnitude: God Himself, Jesus Christ,
has been crucified. He died under Pontius Pilate,
soley because of our sins.

Alas! Jesus says to me, thou hast not yet sounded
the deepest reaches of your sinfulness.
To penetrate such a dark mystery,
You must have a light which comes only from My Heart.

Look upon the Heart which thou hast transpierced, says the
    Holy Ghost.
In as far as you have not understood the love of My Heart,
just so much do you fail to understand the full horror of your
    sins.

No wound of My body on the cross
expresses the true nature of sin
as exactly as the wound of My Heart.

(77)

What best characterizes sin,

what is most abominable in it,

is that it wounds the Heart of Jesus, the Heart of God.

I wish, My child, that you would meditate fondly on

this truth which needs cause you confusion.

How can you think of it without trembling and weeping?

What you see in My pierced Heart

is not only My mercy,

pardon, absolution, purification,

the water which cleanses and the blood which redeems,

graces which withhold you from despair

and from losing the peace of the children of God.

You see also the transplendent reason

why your sin is an odious injury to the love of God,

and an insupportable ingratitude.

For My pierced Heart says to you: I have so loved men

that I have voluntarily suffered for them

a horrible Passion. And yet

that does not keep you from rejecting My love,

from preferring to the living water of My love

the fetid water of unwholesome cisterns.

Sin is always a preference of the heart;

it is the act of a friend who betrays his Friend.

Sin is always against love,

against the love of the Beloved,
against the love of the one Spouse.

No doubt, in the abstract, things are different.
In truth, after the death of Jesus Christ, it is the bride's refusal
of the loving fidelity of the bridegroom.
It is something vile and disgusting:
for a Friend who is so good and who has suffered so much.

I did not expect that of you,
of you, My child, My brother, My chosen one,
of you whom I have not only showered with royal gifts,
but to whom I have shown such tender care,
seeking encounters with you that I may love you more,
giving you My cross to bear, that you may be more united
     with Me.
All My Heart, all My blood, all My innermost being
is shocked by your sin which repulses me.
All My crucified flesh is torn into shreds by it.

No, sin is not simply a mistake,
a mental calculation badly made;
it is a drama of love, because I love men
even to the point of dying for them.
If My Heart had not been pierced by their ingratitude,
sin would not be so intolerable to My Heart.

It would merit hell, but it would not have tortured My Heart
   to that degree.
It is necessary to understand My Heart to understand the full
   gravity of sin.
That is why My Mother understood better than anyone else.

O Jesus, as long as I do not understand
my faults in the light of Thy love,
it is in vain that I pretend to love Thee
with a true love, which you expect from me,
for Thy Heart is a heart pierced by my sins.
There is not another Heart of Jesus.
Neither is there a single sin
which has not wounded Thy Heart for eternity.
Thy Heart and my sins are inseparable;
the record of one and the record of the others form but one.

O Jesus, henceforth I can no longer see my sins
except in the wound of Thy Heart,
nor can I see the wound of Thy Heart
except with eyes purified
by the tears of a sorrowing repentance.
I can no longer have contrition without love,
nor devotion to Thy Heart without contrition.
I can no longer weep over my faults
as a man who is merely ashamed

for having been a bad Christian,
who fears being chastised by divine justice.
My sorrow is deeper and more galling.

It is love which makes me weep
like Mary Magdalen at Thy feet,
like Peter inconsolable for having betrayed Thee, his adored
    Master,
like the prodigal in the arms of his father.
Love's weeping is not that of
disgrace, sadness, grief, selfishness.
Love's tears are matchless:
the whole soul is broken
the whole body is dissolved
the entire being—soul and body—is surrendered
    unconditionally.
As I look upon Thy Heart, I feel myself submerged
in tears of love.
And I no longer know into what ocean I am plunged,
that of my repentance or that of Thy mercy.

XVIII.   What Shall I Render to the Lord

What shall I render to Thee, O Lord, for all the good things
that I have received from Thee? especially for Thy flesh
which Thou hast given me in Holy Communion?
Will it be only a casual "Thank you?"
A few acts of faith, of love, of thanksgiving,
that I shall read, already composed, in a prayer book?
Alas! I see communicants hurrying away
without taking even the time to thank Thee.
Perhaps they consider that to return as quickly as possible to
     their duty
Is to offer the true chalice of praise and to give Thee greater
     glory.
I admit that three or four "Acts after Communion"
are not the only tribute of love which Thou dost expect
from a soul united to Thee through Thy flesh.

To show Thee fitting gratitude
an eternity of adoration will not be too much.

It is impossible, O Jesus, after Mass
to make a thanksgiving worthy of Thee,
having received in Holy Communion
Thy body, Thy blood, Thy soul, Thy divinity.
What shall I render to the Lord for this Communion, for a
   thousand Communions?

—My child, you do not understand the meaning of this
   Sacrament,
and that is why you see nothing else to do but to thank
   Me.
Assuredly, you will never give Me sufficient thanks,
but the purpose of Holy Communion is not
to let you enjoy My sensible presence as you would enjoy
   that of a spouse.
If I wanted to favor you with that pleasure,
I have means other than the Sacrament.
I give you My flesh to eat
in order that you may have a part in My Resurrection
and at the same time in My Redemption and in My mystical
   body.
By faith, hope, and charity
you are made to share in My divine life.
By offering My blood, shed for them, you redeem souls
and you act in the mystical body like Me, with Me,
as a fountain of charity and of union.

You have great work to accomplish

during your thanksgiving; and yet you remain inert

like someone who seems unaware of how much time he is
    losing.

Thanksgiving is an *action,* like the Mass,

an action in which Jesus, Priest in you, desires to fill up

through your hands, what is wanting in the holy Sacrifice.

The Heart of Jesus wishes that the infinite value of the Sacrifice

should pass through your littleness.

It is, then, a time to *act;* it is the privileged hour

of supernatural and apostolic fecundity.

First of all, try to cast yourself into the fire of My Resurrection.

He who has come into you, into your body and into your soul,

is neither dead, nor subject to death.

He is the Resurrection and the Life.

A man who would bathe in fire

or who would swallow a fiery substance

would be no more changed into flames

than the Christian who is nourished with the glorified flesh
    of Christ.

But this flame which assimilates the Christian

to the body of Christ transfigured by the Holy Spirit

far from destroying him as a natural fire would do,

communicates to him the power of His Resurrection.

This fire of the Holy Ghost, at the same time, consumes
all that the fire of purgatory can and must consume.
It cleanses the deepest stains,
those which your conscience does not recognize
and which your will does not reach.
It is the purgatory of love
greater than which nothing can be conceived.

Thanksgiving is the time in which you live
through the sacramental presence in the purgatory of love.
I beg you to dwell for a few minutes at least
In that saving furnace of My Resurrection
and to consign to the flames which penetrate you
your faults, your defects, your bonds, your concupiscences,
all that is opposed to My divine will and to My divine life.

But, after this bath of fire, you will take a bath of blood.
Communion is like a bath in the blood of Jesus.
My child, the priest alone drinks the blood from the chalice
but, like him, you receive My blood, although in a different
       way;
for through the Sacrament you participate in the sacrifice.
You receive My flesh sacramentally immolated.
The unbloody Sacrifice contains the blood which I shed,
and I come into you to pour it on your soul.
Unquestionably, like fire, it purifies you;

but moreover, just as the drop of water is dissolved in the wine,
so your blood is blended with Mine for the redemption of souls.
You become a victim, you become a sacrifice with Me,
and thereby you assume responsibility for the salvation of souls,
the urgent duty of saving them, and at the same time, a re-
    demptory power.

Those who hurry away at the *Ite, Missa est,*
those who communicate outside of Mass,
those who make their thanksgiving idly,
do not understand the exigencies of communion in My blood.
In order that the blood which I have shed may be offered
through you and with you, I instituted the Eucharist.
But for the charge of souls which should occupy your prayer
    for hours,
you can hardly endure ten minutes—
ten minutes to pluck from hell or their slavery
all kinds of souls by the millions.
Ten minutes to meditate on My Passion,
to offer to the Father each of My wounds which are ever open—
would it be too long for your poor heart?

And would not ten more be necessary for the bath of living
    water
of which I am the fountain and which continually gushes out
    in the depth of your soul?
The living water, Saint John tells you, is the Holy Ghost

who is the soul of the mystical body:
he unites all the members of this body of which I am the Head.
The eucharistic Bread nourishes each of these members;
all communicants thus become one single bread.
But this unity, accomplished by Me, must be also your work.
It depends on you that there be a union among Christians
more binding and more extensive.

At holy Mass you have asked
that by your Communion the Church be unified.
Are you the only one you wish to draw to the Church?
Does it not concern all mankind
which by the power of your charity
and by virtue of the desires of Christ in you
you should press forward toward perfect unity?
For you do not communicate for yourself alone
but also, and first of all, for the Church.
To communicate for others is to communicate perfectly.
Does not the word communion remind you of this?
Individualistic thanksgiving fails in part to reach its goal;
I desire an apostolic and catholic thanksgiving.
I desire that the sacaments increase the growth of the Church
and not merely uprooted and isolated individuals.

How can you tell me
that you have nothing to do in your thanksgiving?
If you wish to communicate well,

unite your heart with the Heart of Jesus Christ.

Receive from Him the fire, the blood, and the living water.

Like Him and with Him, open your heart

to the love which He gives you for His Father and for His
brethren.

Spread the fire, spread the blood, spread the living water,

that souls may drink plentifully of the Holy Spirit

in the measure of their good will,

even as you are inebriated by the Eucharist.

XIX.   All That Is Not Love

Divine Heart of Jesus,
preserve me and purify me
from all that is not love of God and of my neighbor
from all prayer that is not of love
from all suffering that is not of love
from all fear that is not of love
from all desire that is not of love
from all trust that is not of love
from all service that is not of love
from all obedience that is not of love
from all humility that is not of love
from all consolation that is not of love
from all terrestrial joy that is not of love
for the Father is Love, the Son is Love, the Holy Ghost
is Love.

Jesus Christ is Love, the Blessed Virgin is love.
Purify me likewise from all love which would be purely
sentiment,

without force, without sacrifice, without self-abandonment.
Grant through Thy Holy Spirit that nothing remain in me
which is not a gift of myself,

    and that every gift of myself may be a gift of Thy love.
Grant that all men, my brothers and sisters in Christ,

    may find in me only Thy love for them.

    Grant that from my stricken heart

    may come forth only the water and the blood of Thy love.

    Make my heart like unto Thine:

    may it be in Thee and through Thee
a source of living water in Thy mystical body,

    a fire, a witness of Thy charity,
and may it spread in all souls

    the unction of Thy Holy Spirit.

XX.   Act of Faith

O my God, I firmly believe all the truths
which the Holy Catholic Church teaches,
because Thou art Truth itself
and canst neither deceive not be deceived.

That is the formula which I have recited since I learned it as
    a child.
No! Lord, Thou canst neither deceive nor be deceived—
that is beyond doubt. I must confess however
that nothing confirms my faith as much as Thy love.
Thy Heart is a treasure house for everything, even for my faith.
If I accept all the truths of revelation,
It is in Thee that I believe, it is Thou who hast revealed them.
But Thou art not only Truth,
thou art also Love, as much Love as Truth.
Thou art not only Love, but Love crucified.
Thou hast a Heart which has been pierced.
Love crucified does not deceive.

If it should deceive, it would not be Love.

It is not possible that Love crucified be not true.

It is sincere, it is loyal, it is given to the very depth.

His blood has been poured out even to the last drop.

There is nothing secret, nothing in it which is hidden.

His Heart is open even to the Holy of Holies.

The veil of the sanctuary has been torn.

It is with the bleeding hands of a martyr

that Thou showest me the ways of truth,

the paths which lead to God.

And all Thy truths are paths

which lead to the Trinity.

Thy charity does not deceive; it shines before my eyes.

It revealed itself for all to see on the cross.

St. John and the apostles saw it and touched it.

They believed in God who died for love.

If, with them, I believe that Thou art Love,

I am certain also that Thou dost conduct me in the
ways of truth.

Thou hast revealed everything through love, O Jesus.

Thou hast said nothing except through love

and for intimate union with God who is Love.

Every one of Thy words is sincere and leads us to
the love of the Trinity.

Ah! if a single word, a single syllable from Thy lips
had not been intended to unite me to God,
thou wouldst not have pronounced it.
Thou didst die for truth.
Thou wouldst not have died if Thou hadst willed to deceive
    me.
That is faith, that is my faith.
I believe because Thou art Truth and Charity.
The Church herself, who is the infallible teacher
of Christian truth,
was born of the pierced Heart of Jesus.
Why was she born of that Heart
if not to show us that she comes from Love
and that she alone leads to Love?
For she alone is born of the Heart of Jesus.
Jesus has only one Church, as the Father has only one Son.

If then I enter her, I enter into the Heart of Jesus;
if I am born of the Church, I am born of the Heart of Jesus,
if I am in her, I am in this divine Heart
which leads to the Trinity.
Outside of her there is no salvation for me.

I trust totally my Mother the Church,
I abandon myself to her direction,
I believe all that she believes and teaches,

because she is the spouse of Jesus crucified,
the new Eve,
united eternally to the Incarnate Word.
That is faith, that is my faith.
To whom, Lord, shall we go?

We believe in the charity of the Father
and in the Heart of Christ who has revealed it to us
and in the Church, His spouse
who, spouse and mother, can neither be deceived nor deceive—
ah! my God, keep me always faithful to the Church!

XXI.   Act of Hope

O My God, relying on Thy infinite goodness and promises,
I hope to obtain pardon of my sins,
the help of Thy grace and life everlasting
through the merits of Jesus Christ, my Lord and Redeemer.

Should I tell Thee, Jesus, that this formula
expresses my hope well, but not entirely?
Through the merits of Jesus Christ? Without any doubt.
But especially through Thy Heart.
For Thy merits are those of love.
A spouse who expects to receive all
the immense fortune of her husband
would be far more happy if she could say:
I expect to receive all from his heart.
His fortune without his heart; a petty treasure; a frail treasure!
His heart without his fortune would be a sure repose.
And if the fortune is given through love,
the spouse then lives in the love of her beloved
in all and for all.

Jesus, it is thus that Thy Heart establishes my hope;
for my hope is not that of a stranger
nor that of a prisoner who awaits his ransom.
My hope is that of a spouse.
Is not my soul truly the spouse of Jesus Christ?
The spouse has her own reasons for hope
to which no one else can lay claim.

As long as my soul is Thy spouse, O Jesus,
and it shall be so eternally,
it is more certain of possessing Thee
and of possessing Thy riches
than if it had complete power over Thee,
save over Thy Heart.
For no heart, much less that of God Himself,
can be forced to give itself.
What can he who is not loved
hope from a heart which is free?

But what can he not hope for
who has been chosen through love
to be eternally united with Christ?
I am assured that my hope
rests on the fidelity of Thy promises.
That is true, especially when they are promises of love.
Fortunately, O Jesus,
Thy promises are in Thy Heart

graven with blood in Thy wounds.
They are one, and one only with Thy Love.
Thy fidelity is Thy fidelity in love;
Thou hast espoused my soul;
everything is included in this covenant.
Through the ages, Thy people had unfailing hope
because of Thy covenant with Israel.

Yet it did not know that this covenant
was Thyself, O Jesus,
Thou, God and Man together,
Thou whose divine blood sealed the New Testament,
Thou who hast given us Thy Holy Spirit
as pledge of our eternal heritage.

Because of that, our hope is no longer an anxious awaiting.
It is no longer a conviction I give myself.
It is already an actual possession of God
in Christ my Brother and the Spirit, His Witness.
The love of Thy Heart has not only promised,
it has given me Jesus, His flesh, His life, His spirit,
and His Resurrection.
And I am assured that Thou wilt give me, O Jesus,
with Thy grace in this world, Thy glory in the next,
if Thou keepest me safe in Thy Heart.

Amen

XXII.   Act of Love

If I content myself with my catechism, here is the formula
of my love for Thee: "O my God, I love Thee
above all things, with my whole heart and soul, and with all
    my strength;
and I love my neighbor as myself
for love of Thee."
God grant that it be so!

Yet, O Jesus, since I have come to know Thy Heart
and its charity for us,
I can no longer love God merely
with my whole heart, with my whole soul, with all my strength.
I know too well, that even if I loved Thee immeasurably
Thou couldst receive from me alone
only a heart unworthy of Thy love.
What is there in me that is not petty, sordid, selfish?
If I had to content myself with loving Thee thus,

my love would be well-nigh agonizing.
My act of love would not leave me happy.
I would not be relieved of the weight of my love.

But, O Jesus, Thou knowest
this helplessness of my heart as well as its anguish.
And through Thy extreme goodness
Thou hast inspired me with a charity more worthy of Thee,
one that fills my soul with joy.

—My brother, My friend, Thou sayest, repeat with me these
    words:
My God, I love Thee with all the love of the Heart of Jesus,
with all the strength of the soul of Jesus.
Repeat it with Me, for your prayer is that of My Spirit
who is in you that you may pray aright.
Your prayer is that of My love which lives in you.
It is that of My blood which makes us "One."
It is that of My grace which has made you a son of God.

With Me, like Me, in Me,
you share in sonship before Our Father.
I have given you all you could receive
of My privileges and of My merits.
Your charity is Our charity; your love, Our love
because I have given them to you.

It is thus that you must love God and pray to Him with Me.
Then it will be with your whole heart,
with your whole soul, with all your strength.
But your insignificant strength will be lost in Mine
as a drop of My blood,
in all the power of My blood.
—O Jesus, how Thy Heart
transfigures my life and my prayer!

My child, learn now how
you should love your neighbor.

You have been told repeatedly: Love him as thyself
for the love of God.
As yourself—that is a great deal.
It is a call to sacrifice.
But that does not sufficiently stir the heart nor raise the spirit.
My Heart has transfigured love of neighbor.
You must love him as I have loved him.
That is the way the Gospel has it.
You must give your life for him,
as I Myself have given Mine.
It is not enough only to imitate My charity.
Perfection consists in becoming the witness
of My charity, the instrument of My charity
through the charity infused in you.

If it is I who in you love the neighbor,
if it is I who give you to the neighbor,
if it is I who sacrifice you for him,
if moreover your charity is Mine,
like to Mine,
springing from Mine as a flame from a fire,
then you have understood the Gospel
and observed perfectly the commandment of the Saviour.
But what a consolation and what an honor
for you and for your neighbor!

You must love your neighbor with My Heart.
Then you can say: I love.
No, it is not I who love
but Jesus who loves in me.

XXIII.   Act of Contrition

Since I have come to know Thy pierced Heart,
O Jesus, the Act of Contrition as I used to recite it,
seems so tepid as to make me doubt
my true repentance, my true conversion.
Simply to regret having offended Thee
because sin displeases Thee
seems too feeble and unworthy of Thy love.

When I see Thy bleeding wounds, my heart
should be torn with grief.
No, Jesus, I no longer want to use a facile formula,
but only to contemplate Thy body a thousand times wounded
and Thy Heart opened by the lance.
Because of my sins,
I want to bury myself, as Thou Thyself hast done,
in bottomless sorrow.

Contemplating Thee crucified, Thy flesh in shreds,
I learn to hate my guilty life.

Each sacred shred represents sin.
My own are spelt out in Thy flesh.
I see what remorse should do with my soul,
a soul in which the wounds of sin
should burn like fire,
healed though they are by Thy blood, my Jesus.

No, I will no longer say that I only displease
Him whom I myself have placed on the cross.
The sight of Thy crucified flesh
Proves to me that Thy death, O Jesus,
is my work and Thy Heart has bled
through me and for me.

And I learn besides, in contemplating Thee,
that my sin forms only one with all the sins of the world,
that it is evil, like the sins of other men,
that all together we have struck Jesus to death
and that my soul, enlightened as it has been, is no less
    responsible
for this crucifixion and for this pierced Heart.
It is a mystery of evil.

O Jesus, I want to bring to Thee in the sacrament
something more than my contrition.
If I do not bear the guilt of all, at least

I want to have sorrow for all—
for all those who have none.
Does not Thy Heart, pierced for everyone, merit
a universal and entire reparation? Men will never have contrition equal
to Thy infinite mercy.

But, Jesus, I hear Thee ask me for an increase of love:
will you, in return for the pardon which I grant you,
for the purity with which I clothe you
repair with My blood the sins of all?
Will you share the sentiments of My Heart
in regard to sinners with whom you were associated?
Will you, in their place, ask for the grace of mercy?
Will you suffer, humiliate yourself, and make satisfaction for
them?
Will you put yourself in My place for them?

Not alone, that would be useless, but with Me?
Will you pray to the Father with My grief and your grief?
That He may pardon them, wash them in My blood,
draw them to Me by virtue of My Passion,
that they may be My brothers and your brothers,
all children of the Father of mercy?

In the Sacrament of penance, I direct to you a double appeal:
that of your contrition and that of your reparation.

(104)

Ah! if, as you are weeping over your sins, you offer and suffer
with Me for the sins of others,
uniting yourself to My agony and My crucifixion,
how fully will you experience the sentiments of My Heart.

And is not this why
I have instituted the sacrament of love,
the sacrament of the reparatory Passion,
the sacrament in which souls are purified
by the blood which I have shed for them?

XXIV. Only One Thing is Necessary

Thou hast proclaimed, Jesus,
that Thy yoke is sweet and Thy burden light.
Light for Thee, O Heart, ever eager for love.
There is no doubt about that.
Thy cross, so heavy on Thy mangled shoulders,
Thy scourging, Thy crowning with thorns, Thy crucifixion,
that heavy weight, crushing for human strength,
was still light for Thy Heart,
because the strength which bore it all in Thee was love.
It was the will of Thy Father passionately embraced,
it was Thy desire to realize the new Pasch.
A desire stronger than the death of a God.

Everything is light for a Heart like Thine—I believe it.
And I have read in the Exercises of Saint Ignatius
that Thy love was so ardent
that Thou wouldst have willed to suffer more. I readily believe
    so.
Yes, for Thee, yes, Thy yoke was sweet and Thy burden light.

But who among us can say as much?

I do not speak of those who carry their *own* yoke,

as a deadly bondage,

but of those who bear *Thine*, Jesus, the yoke of Thy law,

of Thy commandments, of Thy demands, of Thy holiness,

of Thy displeasure, of Thy judgment, of Thy sanctions.

How many of them do I see who are sad, discouraged,
    frightened,

because of their faults, because of Thy chiding glance.

Does there not come forth from Thy mouth a sharp two-edged
    sword

which pierces and torments them?

And to those who have received Thy peace,

O Jesus, Thou hast given a sting

which cuts them; it is the sting of their own wills.

Ceaselessly Thou askest them to be saints.

But Thou and Thy Father, who have filled them with graces,

and the souls for whom Thou hast made them responsible,

complain that they remain mediocre.

Resolved to be perfect, they work

with an unflagging energy;

but their resolutions lose their strength,

their progress is slight,

they give up hope when they see themselves so mean,

so slow, and so useless in the service of their neighbor.

Have I ever met a soul
who finds sanctity easy
and the effort to gain it hazardless?
No, the yoke of Thy will is not light for them.

My child, Thou answerest, prayer especially demands listening.
It is by listening that one gets closest to My thought.
To all souls who groan under the heavy weight of My burden
repeat the word which I spoke to Martha:
Martha, Martha, you are anxious and troubled about many
    things,
And yet only one thing is necessary.
    It is Mary who has chosen the better part.

There are two ways: that of trouble and that of peace.
The first is that of the many things which are added up or
    measured off.
The second is that of people who love.
When one counts his acts of virtue and his faults as he counts
    his money,
when he measures the perfection of his soul
as he measures the height of his body,
when one esteems himself more or less united to God
according to the value of his acts and merits,
when one reckons up his spiritual gains
as laborers harvest fruits;

in short, when one imagines that his resemblance with God
results from a comparison between the being of the creature
and the infinite being of God,
and that the holiest man is he who is nearest God
by the greatness of his being,
then he takes the way of Martha.
Then he is troubled by the excessive bustle and preoccupation
of a virtue which is minded that nothing be wanting
to the Lord Jesus' repast.

But if you abandon the line of being
to follow only that of love,
as I, your Master and Lord, who could
without rapine live as God,
but who, through love, preferred the condition of a slave;
if you seek in all things only to love,
only to give yourself, to serve, to bear the burdens of others;
if you never look for your perfection in the mirror,
but only for the chance which offers itself
of responding in charity
to all the needs of your neighbor;
if you are happy in the evening when God
has given you the grace to love unreservedly,
even though His blinding light shows you
your nothingness, your weakness of will,
the malice within you, your daily faults,

then you can say, as I do, that "My yoke is sweet
and My burden light."
No longer will you feel weighing on your frailty
the burden of My holiness and of My justice,
but that of My love which lives within your soul,
whose flame can consume all the weight of the created world.

How can you imagine that you will be like God,
Except through love?
Like Our Lord, if not through love?
But, in the love which the Holy Ghost communicates to you,
there is such a gift of yourself that your will
and that of God are made one.
Why should you not be perfect as your Father is perfect?

It is love which renders man like to God.
Only love gives the strength of God.
For God does not take away my nature,
he takes away my weakness by giving me His love,
the love of the Priest and the Victim who carried the cross,
who died after saying, "I thirst."
O Jesus! grant that love may make me find sweet and light
the immense burden of the redemption of souls
which Thou hast asked me to carry with Thee
and which Thou dost call Thy "yoke."

XXV. Her Part Shall Not Be Taken Away from Her

"Mary hath chosen the best part
which shall not be taken away from her."
By these words, dear Jesus, Thou didst open the eyes of Martha
and those of the soul which grows weary while working for
    Thee.
If Martha had not needed a lesson,
Thou couldst have sent Mary to help with the table,
and such service would not have taken away her part
which was better than that of her sister.

For, Jesus, Thou art not a man
who hungers and thirsts for earthly food;
Thou dost hunger for other nourishment, that of the will of
    the Father.
Thou art the Incarnate Word.
Thou art not a prophet who gives life
on the condition that his own feeble life be nourished.
Thou art the Resurrection and the Life.

No, Thou hast no need to be served
like a weak and famished man,
nor even like a God who relishes the fragrance
of flesh offerings and bloody sacrifices.
Thou hast need of nothing
except that we receive Thy life, for Thou art Life,
which Thou givest through love.
Martha would have been blamable in doing nothing.
Mary would not have been guilty in laying the cloth
and preparing the supper and the table.
Inactive, Martha would not have received the better part,
and Mary, in her activity, would not have lost it.
For the better part is neither to rest nor to labor;
it is to believe that Thou art the bread of life,
and that it has need only of our love and of our adoration.

No, nothing, nothing, nothing, all creation
is nothing. Jesus, Thou hast need of nothing.
For Thou hast all, Thou art all.
Thou dost possess the Father and the Spirit
as a Son equal to the Father and to the Spirit.
But Thou dost look for my love
because Thou art my God,
because Thou art my life,
because Thou art my resurrection,
because Thou art He who gives all,

and to whom can be given only what has been received from
    Thee.

Whoever loves thus,
knowing that the only hunger and the only thirst
from which Thou sufferest are the hunger and the thirst of
    Thy Heart,
the more he loves, the more he appeases this hunger
and this thirst of Jesus.
If he loves more in praying, let him pray.
If he loves more in working, let him work.
If he loves more in serving, let him serve; in suffering, let him
    suffer.
If he loves more in keeping silence, let him keep silent.
If he loves more in speaking, let him speak.
Everything depends on the will of the Father
for Thy sole nourishment is what pleases Thy Father.

Jesus, the love which Thou givest us
is a love which is very pure, but very active.
For it is the very love of Thy Heart.
It is a gift, a gift of each minute,
and a total gift.
Provided that I give myself, living in Thy love,
whatever be the visible sacrament of this love,
I am assured that I have the better part,

and that it will not be taken away from me.
For my life may be snatched away,
but never the love which is in me,
because it is in Thee, the Resurrection and the Life.

XXVI.   The Mother of Jesus the Priest

O Mother of the Priest Jesus, I wish to thank you
for the most precious gift that you have granted us.
Your benefits are certainly numberless;
no one can count them.
But the greatest of all is often unrecognized:
the gift of the priesthood of Jesus Christ.

For if Jesus, our Brother, were not also our Priest;
if the humanity which you gave Him
had not, in you, received from the Holy Spirit
the unction of the priesthood;
if your immaculate body and blood
had not become, by the ineffable assumption of the Word,
the body and the blood of the one Priest
and of the one Victim of the New Testament,
into what paganism and what materialism
we would have fallen little by little!

But you, O Mary, have saved everything:
the past and the future, time and eternity.
For, O incomparable Mother, thanks to you,
we have in Jesus the one perfect Priest,
the Priest who will not die for all eternity,
the Priest who alone is minister of all churches,
both of the earthly temple and the heavenly sanctuary,
the Priest present in all priests of all time,
giving to each, dignity, authority, and influence,
and absolute power over the bread and the wine,
over all the sacraments and over consciences,
the Priest whom my faith finds the same in all places and at
    all times.
Ah! Does not this celestial gift which you have made us, O
    divine Mother,
surpass all others?
It contains them all, as the sun contains its rays.

But now you grant me a fresh favor: in your charity
you invite me to share in your privilege
as Mother of Jesus the Priest.
You appeal to me to provide for the perpetuity
and the sanctity of the Priesthood of Jesus Christ.
Mother of Jesus the Priest, you are proposing to me to take
    you as model.
What an admirable vocation! What a favor! What an ideal!

It is true, Jesus did not hold priesthood from you
as the Jewish priests held it from Aaron.
The priesthood of your Son was not like His nature,
transmitted through human generation.
It came directly from the Holy Spirit.
Yet, you were the auxiliary
of His eternal and divine priesthood,
the spiritual and necessary auxiliary.
Oh! not merely according to the manner of a servant
or of a minister or of an acolyte,
to give Him material help in His office,
but auxiliary in the very transmission of the unction
through which, right from His birth, the Holy Spirit Himself
    consecrated
His humanity,
the necessary auxiliary of that divine consecration
through which the eternal Father said to Jesus: Thou art My
    Son;
it is I who have begotten Thee this day.

O Mother of the Incarnate Word,
is it not primarily for a similar collaboration
that you have chosen me, me who am nothing,
to serve Jesus the Priest
in all those who have received His priesthood?
You ask me to participate, by my prayers and sacrifices,

in the spiritual maternity of Mary
toward all those whom God has chosen
to be priests of Jesus Christ.

O Mary, give me divine light
to realize profoundly my vocation in the mystical body.
Grant that I may see its depths,
its dignity, its beauty, its fecundity
in the light of your maternity.
Give me the heart of a mother, like yours.
You have received into your heart
the whole heritage of virtues, longings,
and worship of the ancient priesthood.
When the archangel Gabriel carried back to heaven your *Fiat*,
the Word found in you a heart to the image of His own,
an immaculate heart filled with the charity
of the High Priest for all humanity.

Ah! grant that my heart may be filled with charity like yours,
that it too may be completely priestly,
ready to beget in the Holy Spirit,
through prayer and sacrifice,
consecrated members of Christ the Priest,
numerous and saintly priestly vocations.
Grant that not only the priest of my parish
but all children of Mary called to the priesthood

may be the children of my prayer and of my charity.
Grant that all the priests of the entire world, of whatever color,
may be for me and through me other Jesus-Christs,
that I may look upon them and venerate them as Mary
looked upon and adored Jesus in His priesthood.

Holy Mary, Mother of Jesus, give me a heart like yours,
a pure heart filled with the Holy Ghost,
a heart which serves Christ in all His priests
with a limitless devotion and entire forgetfulness of self
for the greater fecundity of the Church.

XXVII.   Act of Trust

Sacred Heart of Jesus, I place my trust in Thee.

I am confident that I shall receive from Thy Heart
torrents of grace and of mercy,
to lead us to the Father, and to increase His glory,
the strength to accomplish all Thy wishes in my regard,
and the realization of all Thy designs on my life.
I can lose everything, even grace,
but never—even until death—shall I lose this confidence,
for it is in Thee and not in my strength that I trust,
and it is impossible to hope for too much from Thy Heart.

I do not wish to rely
either on my strength or on Thy gifts themselves.
Some people say: My trust is the fatherhood of God.
Others: My trust is my persevering prayer.
Others again: My trust is my trust itself.
As for me, my trust is all that
and something which moves me even more.

My trust is Thy Heart.
A Heart like Thine, O Jesus, cannot deceive anyone,
even the most hardened criminal.
And if everything gives way for me and in me,
Thy Heart will remain immutably the same for me,
the pierced Heart of Jesus crucified.

In my misery, my confidence is Thy Heart,
divinely rich in merits;
in my weakness, my trust is Thy Heart,
all powerful and generous.
In my sins, my trust is Thy Heart,
infinitely merciful;
in my selfishness, my trust is Thy Heart,
burning with love even to the folly of the cross.
In my prayer my trust is Thy Heart,
pouring out filial tenderness for the Father.
In my charity my trust is Thy Heart
filled with Thy spirit of love;
in my zeal, my trust is Thy Heart
devoured with the desire to save souls
by Thy precious blood.

By Thy Holy Spirit
Thy Heart is mine
and in me
always and in all things.

I am assured that in it I shall infallibly find
all that is wanting in mine;
the resemblance to Thy Heart
and to that of our immaculate Mother,
the redemption of souls,
the reparation of all sins,
and the greatest glory of the blessed Trinity
in whom my sole eternal wish will be:
through Thy pierced Heart to live and to die.

Amen

XXVIII.   Grant Me A Priestly Heart

My child, Jesus says to me,
I would like to make you an incomparable gift,
greater, more beautiful, more elevated
than any you have ever received up to this very day.
I have given you a heart with which to love God.
And—in order that you may love Him with the same love as I,
with the same spirit—
I have given you the heart of a child of God,
a heart inundated by divine grace.

Now, I would like to raise you
to a more perfect resemblance to **Me**.
I wish to make your heart a priestly heart.
It is only as the fruit of long meditation
that you will measure the depth of this mystery,
for of all the favors granted to My apostles,
it is the richest and the most difficult to comprehend.

(123)

A single example will suffice to excite your attention:
My Mother Mary, the Blessed Virgin, did not receive the
    priesthood.
She did not exercise the functions of Saint John,
but she had to an eminent degree the heart of a priest,
more profoundly priestly than that of Saint John.
Certainly nothing is more exalted than the priest,
and yet if he has not a priestly heart,
like that of Jesus and of Mary,
I do not think he is very pleasing to God,
nor worthy of the spouse of Christ,
nor very useful in the Redemption.
The offering of the co-redemptress
included those of all priests together.
It saved more souls than that of Saint John.
Then, ask My Mother and My Father in My name
to give you a priestly heart like hers
and to teach you little by little the virtue of this great grace.

There is a prayer which you like to recite
because it has such a charming appeal:
"Holy Mary, Mother of God, keep my heart childlike,
pure and transparent as a fountain.
Obtain for me a simple heart which does not savor sadness,
splendid in self oblation, tender to compassionate,
a faithful and generous heart which never forgets a kindness

and holds no resentment against injuries.
Give me a heart which is meek and humble,
loving without asking for return,
joyful in effacing itself in the heart of another
for the sake of Thy divine Son,
a heart great and invincible,
that no ingratitude may close,
that no indifference may weary . . ."

My child, this limpid prayer
disposes you to one more profound.
It is My will that you mount the heights;
do not fear to pray according to My wishes:
Holy Mary, Mother of Jesus the priest,
grant me a priestly heart,
like that of Jesus as a child,
of Jesus at the presentation in the Temple,
of Jesus at the multiplication of the loaves,
at the wedding feast in Cana; at the Pasch in the Cenacle,
of Jesus in the agony and before Annas and Caiphas,
and especially of Jesus on the cross
when He expired giving up the ghost.

Grant that I may be able,
with the priestly Heart of Jesus,
with the same love and the same intentions,

without separating myself from Him,
to love the Father in heaven and all His creatures,
to offer the only sacrifice which honors Him,
which glorifies Him, which reaches His mercy,
which repairs and effaces sins.
Grant that I may be able with Him
to love men and especially sinners
without pharisaism, with a charity entirely pure,
and a total forgetfulness of myself.

I want to run, like the Good Shepherd,
after the sheep that has strayed,
that all may hear His voice when I call them,
that the sentiment of the hireling may never infiltrate my heart,
in fine that I may give my life for souls,
for the flock of Christ which is the Church.
Holy Mary, Mother of Christ, grant me, then, a priestly heart,
a heart which experiences the sentiments of Jesus
and which is purified of all which does not proceed from
His eternal priesthood.

I ask this of Thee not only for myself
but for all the priests of Jesus Christ
to whom I lovingly offer my help—
all those priests who in reality have only one priesthood,
that of Jesus Christ,

all those priests, each of whom is Christ,
and possesses all the power of Christ
over His eucharistic and mystical presence in the Church.

O Jesus, give them a powerful grace
that their hearts may live in intimate union with Thy Heart,
that they may celebrate the holy sacrifice, absolve sins,
preach Thy word, convert the unbelieving,
recite the Divine Office, immolate themselves with the sacred
    Host,
with a heart which Thy priesthood
has flooded with the unction of Thy holy spirit
and inflamed with the fire of Thy infinite love.

In their ministry, may men experience more and more
the charity of a Curé d'Ars,
of a Vincent de Paul, of a Francis de Sales,
of a Xavier, of a Regis, of so many others,
in whom, souls urged on by the Holy Spirit
have found a priestly Heart like Thine.

—My child, I will show you to what heights your desires,
your requests, your service must rise.
Continue always to pray for My priests
for their priesthood depends on the prayers of the faithful.
But I am happy that you have had the courage

to ask for a priestly heart for yourself also.

Excellent as it may be, your heart will not be truly like Mine, united to Mine, consumed in love,

unless it be impressed with the image of My priesthood.

Little by little, I will unveil to you the beauty of this image.

XXIX.   The Prayer of My Heart

Jesus, teach me to pray.
It seems to me that anything is easier to me
than to talk with Thee, than to hold with Thee
a conversation in which Thou listenest to me
and in which I listen to Thee, each of us present to the other.
Even though I should be able to love, to work, to suffer,
to practice all virtues,
I should still feel incapable of praying a long time
because my spirit so often wanders far from Thee, and my
     heart is so dry.

—My child, there are difficult prayers
taught by men.
The easiest and best prayer
consists simply in praying with Me.
For, because of My eternal priesthood,
I Myself pray forever.
I have prayed since My birth, and I will never cease

to pray, because I shall never cease to be the sovereign Priest
of all creation.

My priestly Heart is one whose love
glorifies the Father by the offering of its merits.
All the days of My mortal life
I offered prayers and supplications
accompanied by great cries and tears,
and I was heard for My piety.
And all that remains for eternity.
I possess a priesthood which does not pass away.
I am able to save all men
who come to God through Me,
for I am always living to intercede in their favor.

The best prayer, the only worthwhile prayer,
is the prayer of the great High Priest and eternal Mediator
whom the Father has chosen for Himself.
If you wish to pray perfectly, My child,
you must pray with Him, in His name, in His person,
with His priestly Heart.

Recall what I said in all solemnity to My disciples:
amen, amen, I say unto you.
If you ask the Father anything in My name,
He will give it to you.

Ask and you shall receive that your joy may be full.
Then I added that this joy which could not be taken away
    from them,
would begin with the Resurrection:
on that day, you will ask in My name.
For on that day, the prayer will be that of the risen Christ.
When I shall have returned to the Father
all that you will ask in My name, I will do,
in order that the Father may be glorified in the Son.
If you ask Me anything in My name, I will do it—
a wholly new prayer addressed to the Father in the Son,
and to Christ who is in the Father,
and which both must hear and grant.

To pray in a perfect and efficacious way,
you must place yourself in the presence of God,
with Him who has already entered into the Holy of Holies.
You can do it with absolute confidence.
Thou hast not approached, said the Apostle,
an untouchable reality, nor a burning fire,
nor dark clouds, nor shadows,
nor the resounding trumpet, nor that voice
so powerful that they who heard it begged
that they should be spoken in such wise no more.
All that is ended, ended, ended. Have confidence!
You have come to the city of the living God,

(131)

the heavenly Jerusalem, and to the company of many thousands
    of angels,
and to the church of the firstborn who are enrolled in the
    heavens,
and to God, the judge of all,
and to the spirits of the just made perfect,
and to Jesus, mediator of a new covenant,
and to a sprinkling of blood which speaks better than Abel.
Thou art with Jesus close to the Father—that is priestly prayer.
Confidence, confidence, confidence.

How simple is this prayer which has already been made by
    Jesus,
through the priestly Heart of Jesus.
Would you wish to substitute another prayer?
Priestly prayer is simple, poor, and humble,
possessing nothing of self, having all from Jesus;
a prayer of great power,
because its value comes from the offering of His Heart.
If you make this prayer, you know how to pray,
for you possess the very source of all prayer.
You can lose yourself in adoration without words and without
    ideas;
you can praise, thank, offer, ask;
you can meditate on all the words of Jesus of Nazareth,
all the actions of His life, a life near to the people.
You can consider in detail the countless needs

of sinful men, for whom Christ died.
You can read or chant the Office,
participate in the visible Liturgy.
The object of human thought matters little;
provided that, with a priestly heart
you are one with the eternal Priest,
your prayer is excellent and all-powerful.
And so simple! and so silent!
For it is Jesus who prays with you and in you.

My Lord Jesus, listening to Thy words,
simply listening to the beatings of Thy Heart,
I have felt that my heart really prayed,
as if an echo prolonged Thy interior voice within me.
Yes, our souls really pray
when they are united to Thee,
when through love they offer to the Father
Thy thoughts, Thy gifts, Thy supplications, Thy merits,
and especially the love of Thy priestly Heart.
Ah! how easy Thou hast made prayer for us!
Nothing, either in action or in prayer,
can hinder us from associating ourselves
with the heavenly offering of the one eternal Priest
through faith in Thy priesthood at the right hand of the Father.
O my God and Saviour, how delightful a duty prayer becomes
when one can pray with Thy Heart.

XXX.   The Joy of My Heart

Lord Jesus, I find it very difficult
to will to associate myself with Thy priesthood.
I am really afraid of such an exalted grace;
for priesthood to me is a sign of sacrifice,
of voluntary, constant sacrifice;
the daily state of victim repels me, for I am weak.
I have neither the strength nor the desire to submit myself
        to it.

How dark is your faith—Jesus says to me.
In all things you see first what will be the cost to you,
and you do not perceive what will bring you happiness.
It is true that a heart cannot be priestly
if it does not share all the sufferings of the world,
which are *My* sufferings.
But neither is it priestly
if it does not participate in all the joys of the risen Christ.

In his triumphant Epistle to the Hebrews, My child,
the Apostle accurately described My priesthood.

We have a High Priest, he said, who in heaven
sits at the right hand of the Throne of the Majesty of God.
He is there in the quality of Minister
of the true sanctuary and the true tabernacle,
raised by the Lord and not by man.

Up to the coming of Christ, everything was earthly.
Since He came, all is heavenly: priesthood, tabernacle,
altar, liturgy, victim, offering.
My priesthood, linked to My sonship,
is consummated, exalted, eternalized
by My Resurrection. Through My Resurrection there is full
    realization of
My work as mediator, the glory which I render to My Father,
the efficacy of My assiduous prayer, and
the redeeming power of My Passion.

And the Apostle, recalling the images of the ancient Temple,
was inspired to say; By my own blood,
I entered once for all into the Holy of Holies,
procuring thus an eternal Redemption.
But it was absolutely necessary to enter into the Holy of Holies
by the shedding of My blood.

My disciple, the Beloved John, contemplated Me
in the heavenly Jerusalem

as a Lamb which had been slaughtered,
which is at the same time, the Lion of Juda
and the warrior who conquered the Beast,
holding in His hand the destinies of the world.
That means, My fearful child,
that My priestly Heart is a Heart flooded
with glory, power, and goodness,
a Heart whose love is victorious
and one which no longer experiences the agonies of earth.
It is filled with the plenitude of life
which henceforth, through virtue of My Passion fully con-
    summated,
it can pour out at will
into an infinity of members of My mystical body.

He is worthy, the Lamb who has been slain,
to receive power, wisdom, riches,
strength, honor, glory and benediction.
A priestly heart in the image of Mine
must participate in all My privileges
especially in My joy, My victory,
My mercy, My power, and My triumph.
Ah! certainly, for the present it is through faith;
but if you live according to faith, your heart
will be exalted and be raised above the earth,
by the power of My priesthood.

Oh! Jesus, I am confounded by Thy greatness of soul,
by the graces which Thou dost manifest to me
in giving me a heart like Thine.
I see it in Thy words, O Jesus;
a priestly heart is a royal heart,
a heart filled to overflowing with celestial joy,
indeed a heart which does not let itself be overcome by trials,
which reigns over all the agitations of this world,
a heart which sadness does not weaken,
which suffering never discourages,
a heart which lives in heaven with Thee
victorious over all its enemies, Thy enemies,
glorifying the Father in uniting itself to Thy Passion,
a heart which has found in Thy Resurrection
peace, serenity, joy, trust,
the sources of that river of life where souls
refresh themselves to satiety in its purifying waters.

Ah! Who, if not Thou, O Jesus, who art infinitely happy,
will give me a heart like Thine
for the most complete happiness of creation?

XXXI.   The Thirst of My Heart

Dear Lord, is it necessary for Thee to explain to me
why Thou didst say on the cross, "I thirst?"
A thousand voices including that of the Church have repeat-
    edly told me
Thou didst speak of Thy thirst for souls.
It was not a torture of the body
but a cry from Thy Heart
which made Thee call: Help Me!
Help Me in My love for souls.

During Thy cruel Passion,
Thou didst never complain of Thy too great suffering.
No affront, no whiplash, no tearing of Thy flesh
had wrenched from Thee the cries of a man being tortured.
But Thy thirst for souls was stronger
than all the cruelty of the executioners.
Thou didst cry out because Thy love for souls
sought to move our hard hearts,
the hearts of men of all time.

(138)

Thy cry was not that of the Son of God
who had no need of any creature
since He had His Father;
but the cry of the Priest who wishes to save souls.
The Virgin, Thy Mother, was the first to hear it.
When Thou didst ask her to be the Mother
of all sinful men, she did not hesitate to help
to quench Thy thirst for the redemption of all men.
She adopted them all, even the executioners
for she had a priestly heart
like Thine.

O Jesus, how sad and revolting it is
to hear people assert that no one can be damned,
that there is no serious danger of being lost.
Our Lord would have suffered and cried out for something of
    little import,
The tragedy of salvation would have ended with Him.
The responsibility of our priesthood would not be of much
    concern,
priests could let matters run their course,
the Blessed Virgin herself would no longer be the refuge
of vile and desperate men.
No one would have need of that last hope,
a final recourse to Mary.

The *Sitio* of Jesus resounds even into eternity.
Any mother would utter a cry if she saw her child
fall into the fire. She would throw herself
into the flames to snatch him out.
Jesus was the victim of a similar but more vehement love;
for all the sinners of the earth
He sounded the alarm of His dying Heart.
The love of Thy Heart, O Jesus,
is a love which gives us the folly of the cross.
Thy eternal priesthood burns with a love
more painful than the thirst of a wounded man
who has shed all the blood from his veins.
It inflamed the hearts of the apostles with a consuming zeal.
They likewise died from exhaustion,
crucified by sinners, their hearts pierced by grief.
"Sinners have killed the sinner,"
said the Curé of Ars when he was about to die.
The zeal of Thy Heart, lighted in his priestly heart,
had made him a holocaust of love.

If God had not glorified His mercy
by the reparation of the High Priest, His Son,
priestly agony would not strain our hearts
as it strained that of Jesus all His life.
O Jesus, a Heart like Thine
cannot live as if hell were not a constant menace,

as if there were no sinners, madmen,
rushing helplessly to their ruin.
Such a heart suffers with the same dread that made Thee call
for help when Thou wert dying of thirst—
the dread of seeing souls escape from Thy love,
from Thy bleeding hands, from Thy pierced Heart.

Jesus, shall I dare ask for Thy thirst for souls?
Thou knowest that it is a torture
that would make me cry out in my prayer
and leave me no more rest.
If I thought of those dying each day
as a mother dreams that her son is drowning,
I would have no more tranquility nor ease.

—My child, to this agony, do you prefer the shame
of a selfish life, heedless of souls?
Do you prefer a life without heart and without love?
You will always suffer in life. But do you prefer
suffering that is sterile and of its own nature foolish
to the noble and fruitful suffering of Christ?
If you wish to have a priestly heart
like the Heart of Jesus,
you must have an entire forgetfulness of self
and think only of the salvation of souls,
no longer place your delight in anything but in loving sinners,

delivering them eternally to My priestly love.
Then your heart and Mine will be but one heart
in the flames of the Holy Spirit.

XXXII.   The Priest, My Other Self

The priest, My child, does not mean to you
all that he means to Me.
He never will; because your faith
however lively it may be, will always be weak
and incomplete, intermingled with human views and shadows.
But if you knew all that the priest is to Me,
you would regard him as My other self.

—Lord Jesus, enlighten me. Regarding the priest, I know
all that the Church has taught me.
But I see in him also something which veils to my eyes
the divine face of Jesus Christ.
Thy presence in the Tabernacle is easier to believe
than Thy presence in him who, nevertheless, has consecrated
    the Host
and who has placed it in the ciborium and in my heart.
But Thou tellest me that this mystery of faith
is as dear to Thy Heart as that of the Eucharist.

(143)

—Perhaps, My child, it is more dear
because the appearances of bread are nothing,
while the priest is one of My elect children
whom I have chosen from his birth
and from eternity according to the determination of the
    Trinity,
as an extension of My priesthood,
a remembrance and an instrument of My Passion,
a living expression of My charity,
an effusion of the Holy Spirit in the Church,
another form of Incarnation of Myself.
I had the condition of God; I took that of a slave;
and now I have taken the priestly form.

I love the priest, not only as something useful to My ends,
but somewhat as I love My own humanity,
the members of My body and of My soul,
and My Mother Mary, who gave Me My humanity.
The Immaculate Virgin gave Me birth.
In his way, the priest is also a mother to Me,
because, through the sacraments, he gives Me a presence
living, active, real, total, matured, fruitful,
a presence of Love among men.

The priest diffuses My divine life in all times
and the multiple fruits of My most powerful Passion,

the fruits of My most powerful and tender love.
Through the Holy Spirit, he gives growth to
My mystical body, as the Virgin gave birth
and fostered My divine body even to its maturity.
And that is why I love the priest, every priest,
in the intimacy of My sacramental life.
If the priest loved Me as much as I love Him,
if he gave Me as much of himself as I give Myself to him,
if he were a sort of eucharistic "species,"
whose bond with me would be a bond of love,
ah, how much better men would know the riches of My Heart.
But many are lacking in faith, and the human, the too human,
       offends and scandalizes them.

I see faithful souls regarding with a supernatural view
churches, altars, sacred vessels, golden crosses,
immaculate linens, all blessed objects.
And yet no material object can have a sacerdotal character.
The priest is infinitely above the temple,
the altar, all the objects of religious worship.
All the holiness of sacred things
flows from his sacramental power and from his dignity.
None of them is Jesus Christ. On the contrary, the priest is
       the extension of Jesus.
In His name, that is to say in His person, he prays, he speaks,
he acts, he absolves, he blesses, he consecrates.

Where faith does not see Jesus Christ in the priest,
there are only images and play-acting for the senses.

Mothers who are honored by having a son ordained to the
    priesthood,
a son who mounts the altar, who gives Jesus to the world,
who blesses them and spreads around him divine life,
only faintly realize the happiness which is theirs.
And the devout souls who pray for priestly vocations,
who foster them, help them, render them possible,
and those, too, who devote themselves to the service of the
    priesthood
in the manner of the Virgin in the service of Jesus,
all these souls, as faith performs in them
the miracle of the Transfiguration and dazzles them
with the simple presence of Jesus Christ,
are privileged by His Heart.
Their vocation profoundly moves the priestly Heart
of Jesus Christ and intimately promotes His love.

Jesus is present in the poor man who stretches out his hand,
in the sick in the hospital, in the wounded Samaritan,
in the child of the street, in the hunted wretch.
But He is much more and by a special unction
in the consecrated priest.
Judas claimed for the poor the 300 denarii

(146)

which Magdalen dispensed to anoint the feet of Christ,
but Jesus praised her for thus honoring His sacred body.
Like Magdalen, the souls who devote themselves to the service
of priests
Render to Christ, through their living faith,
the highest homage and that which is most appealing to His
Heart.

My God, give me a eucharistic and priestly heart.
May the priest always represent to me
Jesus ready and willing to give food
to my soul! If I but knew the gift of God!

XXXIII. Your Life Story Written in My Heart

The complete record of your life, My child, in all its details
and without any possible error, is written
not in your memory, nor in that of others
nor in the mind of the angels,
but only in My Heart.
If My Father did not read it in My Heart,
He would not know it in its entirety.
For to know Me, is to know you.
It is to see you in My love,
in My body, in My wounds, in My blood.

God Himself is not able
to see you where you are not.
But *you* are not where *I* am not.
Just as the eye perceives objects in the light,
God beholds you only in His Word,
in His Christ, beginning and end of creation.

(148)

You partake of My divine sonship;
the Son of the Father has made you a member of His body,
a living member of the Word Incarnate.
God would be imperfect if He judged you
other than you are.
Whatever is good in you,
whatever is pleasing in the eyes of the Father, whatever avails
  unto justice,
is an effect, a gift, a reflection of My love.
I have given your record its origin, its meaning, its end.
It comprises a thousand daily details,
the greater part unperceived or forgotten by men and by
  yourself.
However, the fabric they make up
has been ingeniously woven by My love.

Pluck out a thread from your existence
and I will show you that it has merit
only through My vigilant and active love.
That is why no one can deny
that his record is written in My Heart.

It is fortunate for you that it should be in My Heart,
and not only in your own conscience,
that God should see it unfold hour by hour,
for you relate it to yourself not without pride,

perhaps not without discouragement,
because you regard it as if Jesus Christ
had no part in it. Thus your record is mutilated.

You do not know the gifts of God, nor do you know even your
    sins.
Your sins, of which indeed you are the sole author,
whose entire malice comes from you,
and from you against God,
you do not see in their true perspective.
The record of your sins,
like that of your good actions,
can be read only in My Heart.
Everywhere else it is falsified.
Every confession, in all sincerity, would have to
retell all that My Heart has suffered
and count the invisible wounds of My love.

For if it is true that your sins offend God,
nothing in Him is sensitive or vulnerable
as is the body of Christ, the soul of the Son of God.
But if His body has borne the wounds of our misdeeds,
how much more has His tender Heart!
Are not all our sins opposed
to the love of Jesus, our Brother, our Friend?
Can you imagine all that His love tried to do
before they were committed

to keep you from scorning the infinite goodness
of His Father and that of Jesus crucified?

If the Father and the Son had not loved you,
your sins would not have reached up to Their majesty
nor to Their immutable beatitude.
Sin brings sorrow to God
only in His incarnate Son and in His love.
That is why the record of your guilty life
is written only in My Heart.

And if in your eyes it makes you more hateful
and more to be despised, you will find, however,
in this mystery of ingratitude
a more profound mystery of mercy.
Since your sins are all according to their full reality,
engraved like wounds in My Heart,
who can ever think that they do not find pardon there?
For My Heart is truly a furnace
of mercy; no sin resists that fire.
My Heart is filled with divine blood.
One single drop of the blood is enough
to wash away all possible transgressions.

My Heart is the sanctuary of pardon.
Everything in it is pure in the eyes of God.
It is also the sacrament of pardon.

There is more pardon in My Heart than on My lips,

than in My eyes, than in My arms.

Before you hand over your sins in the sacrament of penance,

the pardon is completely formed in My Heart.

If it is slow to purify you, it is because your repentance is slow.

Repent and your sins will be remitted

for they were already pardoned.

The Father of the prodigal opened his arms

before the child came to him.

The Good Shepherd carried the sheep in his love

before carrying it on his shoulders.

In the Heart of Jesus there is nothing

which is not purified in the flames of love.

The glance of the all-holy God sees no blemishes

in the compassionate Heart of His Son.

—O Jesus, Thy words bring tears to my eyes!

Let me first of all weep in silence.

So much happiness calls forth tears of joy.

Thou makest me weep by telling me that

my sins are hidden in Thy Heart almost before they are
     committed,

as if they were Thy treasure,

relics of Thy sufferings,

a personal glorification which Thy Father would have given
     Thee.

Each of my sins recalls to Thee Thy Passion,
Thy unforgettable sorrows.
Those of the agony, of the scourging, of the crucifixion
are infinitely beloved remembrances
to Thy priestly Heart.
For the justice and the mercy of Thy Father
were fully satisfied,
and Thou didst open to me fountains of blood
in which all the sins of the world are washed.

O Jesus, Thou makest me weep in adoration,
in gratitude, in contrition, in trust.
No, I shall no longer think of my sins
with the bitter gall of wounded pride.
I shall look upon them only where in truth they are,
in Thy priestly Heart,
already pardoned, expiated, repaired,
bathed in Thy superabundant mercy.
I am certain that by the sacrament,
Thou dost pour over me the waves of that mercy.
I wish, henceforth, to confess only to Thy opened Heart,
to count my failings only as wounds of Thy Heart,
and to await only from Thy Heart the absolution of the priest.

XXXIV. The Sanctity of My Heart

My child, all souls know that they must be pure
if they are to have any resemblance to Me.
But there are few who realize
the eminent sanctity which he who wills to have
a priestly heart must acquire.

—Lord! Every day, the Eucharist reminds me
that a priestly heart is a eucharistic heart.
It is nourished with the bread of angels.
It feeds upon Thy divine flesh born of the Immaculate Virgin,
filled with the glory of God and with the virtue of the Holy
    Spirit.
To enter into the banquet hall,
Thou Thyself hast said, one must wear the nuptial robe,
the robe of the spouses of Christ,
the robe washed in the blood of the Lamb.

And I know that by Thy flesh thou dost cleanse
my less than perfect purity and give it an ever increasing
    brightness.

For Thy flesh is a fire of divine glory,
a purgatory of love
whose purifying power
no furnace can equal.
A fire capable of reducing to flames
the most resistant metals,
will never equal the infinite force
of the divine flesh of the Word,
nor will any solvent equal the power of a single drop
of the divine blood
which washes all the sins and all the defilement of the universe.

Plunged each morning through the sacrament of Thy risen
    body
into the glory of the Holy Spirit,
as into a bath of brilliant light,
my heart, always stained and flawed,
becomes an ever clearer image
of Thy eucharistic Heart, O Jesus.
What thanks I shall render to Thee eternally!

And I know many other things
which give me a hunger and thirst for purity
that all human joy only tends to sharpen.
When I see with what burning eagerness
the bride seeks to please her bridegroom,

the artist, his connoisseurs,
and with what splendor creation was clothed
when it came forth from Thy hands,
how could I live in the presence of my Spouse
with the ugliness of my secret sins?

Besides, all my life as a child of holy mother Church
takes place in the sacrament of Thy priestly presence:
the tabernacle, the ciborium, the chalice,
the sacred linens, the ornaments, the lights,
all the gold and all the precious stones of the Church,
which are the sensible signs of the heavenly Jerusalem,
and especially the priest who bears in himself Thy presence
and who gives me, if I receive it with faith, Thy Word,
Thy will, Thy pardon, Thy grace, Thy Holy Spirit.
I know that I live each day
as in a sanctuary where everything is sacred,
where everything invites me to reverence and to holiness.

—I am going to interrupt you, My child, for you would never
    tire
of telling Me all that My Heart
has liberally bestowed on you,
with the hope that you will have a pure heart
in the likeness of the Heart of Jesus and of Mary
and of all the saints
who have reflected the beauty of My priesthood.

But I wish to show you something better and more beautiful
than all these great favors.
My priestly Heart is pure not only
because it is without sin,
but especially because it is a Mediator.
Its purity is of a divine order.
It is filled with the very sanctity of God.
If you were to study the Holy Bible
to get some idea of the sanctity of God,
sanctity which separates God infinitely from every creature,
you would know of what high perfection I wish to speak.

The purity of My Immaculate Mother
resembles that of My priestly Heart.
But between the sanctity of My Heart and that of her heart
there yet remains a yawning abyss.

I am a priest because I am man
but also because I am God.
My Heart is priestly because it is the Heart of the Word.
The Apostle wrote: The glory of becoming High Priest
has been attributed to Christ by Him who said,
Thou art My Son: it is I who have begotten Thee this day.
Thou art a priest forever according to the order of
        Melchisedech!
And consequently according to divine generation.
And this choice of the Father was accompanied with an oath.

He is the only one who became priest by a solemn promise
    of the Father:
the Lord has sworn it and He will not repent.
Thou art a priest forever.
My Heart would not be priestly
with all the dignity of the angels
nor with that of Abraham, of Moses and of Aaron;
it becomes so by the very divinity which fills it.
It is priestly because the Spirit which consecrates it
is its own Spirit, the Spirit equal to the Word,
the Spirit given to its humanity through the Father and the
    Son.

My Heart is mediator only if it is the Heart of God.
Such is the profound meaning of the priestly character
of My Heart and of My charity.
When I call you to this sublime perfection
of possessing a heart like Mine
without question I ask of you absolute purity,
but I implore something more:
the sanctity of a mediator between souls and God,
the sanctity of a soul united to God,
plunged in God, living in God,
in intimacy with God, in contact with souls.
I ask you to be as living water
which is in the fountain-head and overflows from it

You must be a kind of continuous current
between Jesus and souls,
enlightening them, giving them life.
You can have a pure heart,
but you will never have a priestly heart
if, living with souls, you do not live also in Jesus Christ,
animated by a single love which descends from My Heart
and returns into My Heart to go out again
always more divine, always more ardent, always more
     efficacious.

Oh! Lord Jesus! It will be necessary for Thee
to speak to me over and over again
of that extraordinary holiness of the priestly heart.

XXXV.   The Suffering of My Heart

Since I am going to open My Heart to you
and to make manifest the unctions of My priesthood,
I must tell you of My sufferings
which are unfathomable wounds in My Heart,
lighted by a celestial fire,
by a torrent of flames which keeps them
always opened and always fruitful.

They are priestly wounds
whose burning cannot be compared
with the sufferings of men on earth.
For these latter are the effects of their sins,
and *their* torment is that of their *own* selfishness,
which refuses to sacrifice itself for another.
It is not thus with My wounds of love.

My priesthood is entirely for the good of others.
It brings nothing to Me, for the Word can receive nothing

which is not already the eternal gift of His Father.
It is like a fountain always flowing with gifts,
it is like the light, which exists only in shining.
My priesthood is the door through which God
passed to die "outside the camp."
He, so to speak, went out of it to enable His creatures to share
    in His divinity
by communicating to them the Holy Ghost.

That is why suffering in My priestly Heart
does not destroy the happiness of loving, but exalts it.
It is not like the sorrows of men.
Before My Resurrection, I felt an unspeakable torture,
but that torture was supported and transfigured by love;
My Heart never knew suffering greater than love
even in My agony, even in prison, even on the cross.
After My Resurrection, there remained nothing but the exulta-
    tion of love
and the ineffably sweet reminder
of My sacrifice for love.

If you wish to have a priestly heart
like Mine at this present time,
you must purify the selfishness which overwhelms you,
and you must suffer only for others.
Your suffering, filling up what is wanting

to My redemptive Passion
will complete the work of My eternal priesthood.

Then what joy will fill your heart, united with Mine
in the midst of troubles of all kinds.
For My priesthood is in heaven!
By sacrificing yourself for another,
you will taste the joy of following the Lamb that was
　　immolated,
the joy of generous love which gives itself,
the joy of the Resurrection of Christ,
who lives now in your sufferings
as He formerly did in His own,
the joy of uniting with Him in the salvation of souls.

No, the priestly heart cannot suffer
like a heart alone in the night,
uselessly and in the dark.
It should suffer in order to enter soul and body,
enlightened by faith, into the Holy of Holies,
with the blood of Christ and the sign of the cross,
and in order to lead thither trusting souls.
Then it tastes profound delight
in knowing that its suffering is not so much its own
as that of the eternal Priest
who has conquered the world and consummated the Pasch.

—Lord Jesus, grant that my heart
may not be attached to the satisfactions of this world,
to all that would make me forget the unfortunate.
Jesus, High Priest of all mankind,
as Thou hast taken on Thyself all the sorrows of the world
and all the horrible sins of all time,
desiring to expiate them and to atone for them through Thy
    sacrifice,
grant me the grace to have a universal love
and to draw from my union with Thy priestly Heart
sufficient strength to be willing to suffer
with the joy of Thy Resurrection.

But is it true, O Jesus, that Thou art completely happy?
Hast Thou not confided to certain souls
that Thou needed to be consoled in Thy sorrows,
as if we were present at Thy Passion?
I said that, My child, as I said to Saint Paul:
why do you persecute Me?
And to those on My right: What you have done
to the least of Mine,
you have done unto Me.
Suffering is a sort of sacrament.
Men bring hither the bitter fruit of their sins
and I bring My Resurrection
and all the fruits of My Passion.

And that is why they live in Me and I suffer in them.
We are both present in this sacrament.
My Passion is certainly present, as I am present
in My mystical body.
I say truly that I suffer in you
but you say truly that in Me you are a saviour of souls.
A priestly heart understands that very easily.
I will give you a heart like Mine and you will understand.

XXXVI.   The Chastity of My Heart

Dear child of My priestly Heart,
spouse of My priestly Heart,
sister of Saint John, My beloved,
who was, with My Mother, the privileged witness
of the opening of My Heart by the lance,
and the first Apostle of My redeeming love,
if I speak to you now of the chastity of My Heart,
it is in order to make you experience the divine embrace
which binds and fastens you to My priesthood.

Chastity is not only the avoidance of sin;
it is marriage with Jesus alone,
of which, perfect human marriage is only a symbol.
It is the total and reciprocal gift of the soul and Christ,
sealed by the redeeming blood of the cross.
It is consequently more exalted than all purity.
My Heart is not only pure; it is chaste,
because it is the Spouse of souls

who wish to love it alone
in the royalty of My Priesthood.

The chastity of My Heart is My inviolable covenant
with Israel, My people, My chosen children.
As God I am holy, as Priest I am chaste;
for I am eternally united
with all the children of God whom I have chosen
to save souls with Me through My blood.

The chastity of your heart is a consecration to My priesthood.
You could, My child, be a sinless creature
and yet not be a spouse chosen
to give to My redemption a multitude of children.

My priesthood is the hypostatic union of the Word
with His humanity, eternal, unalterable.
But is is also a mystical union with souls
who by My humanity are called
to produce and to spread the living fruits of My priesthood.
Chastity is a fidelity to My priesthood,
a love exclusive and unshared.

The priest must have a chaste heart
because My sacerdotal Heart lives in him,
and because I am, by My priesthood, Spouse of the Church.

He also can have no spouse but the entire Church.
A priestly heart can love only
the princely gifts and the royal crown,
bought by the most precious blood of Jesus,
which render the creature worthy spouse of the Son of God.

Marriage is only an image of chastity:
the marks of marriage are an image
of the marks of chastity.
The proofs of marriage are an image
of those of chastity.
Just as the wounds of the risen Jesus
show that Jesus suffered His Passion on account of love,
the visible proofs of chastity
show to all carnal eyes
that the heart of the spouse of Christ
belongs only to the pierced Heart of Jesus.

My child, you do not make sufficient account
of the importance to the world of the signs of chastity.
Chastity proclaims with certitude that there is possible,
on this earth, a contract signed
not by the ink of men, but by the blood of Christ.
At the same time it attests that there exists on this earth
a union between souls and the risen Christ
that death does not break,

because it is eternal,
because the priesthood is eternal.

My child, do you wish to render Me this noble service
of witnessing by your chastity,
or at least by your veneration for chastity,
that I am really present here below
and that I espouse souls in divine love?
It is in chaste souls that the splendor of the heavenly Jerusalem
appears in the Church militant through the clouds of faith.

—O Jesus, what great, unhoped-for graces
I was asking when I dared ask Thee:
give me a priestly heart.
When Thou dost inspire a prayer in our souls,
we cannot comprehend all Thy desires;
they infinitely surpass our expectations and our hopes.
More than ever, Jesus, I ask Thee for a priestly heart.

XXXVII.   I Am the Door

I was seeking the door to go to Thee, my Jesus,
to enter into Thy friendship, into Thy love,
in the inmost depths of Thy Heart,
so as to live no more a prisoner of this world,
nor prisoner of myself,
but totally at liberty in Thee,
with the freedom of the Holy Spirit.

That door I had finally found.
It was charity, the charity of Thy Heart.
It pressed me to give for men, my brethren,
all that I had and all that I was.
That is why Thou hast told me that the door is narrow
and that few souls pass through.
But blessed is he who makes himself small enough,
humble enough, even to the dust, to be no more
than a flame of love!
For he easily clears the low door.

Having, as best I could, passed through the door, by charity
    and humility,
I believed that I would henceforth live in Thee and of Thee.
What a deliverance and what beatitude!
Could I suppose that this was not the supreme happiness?
But today Thou speakest to me
as if beyond Thyself there were still something to be sought
or some one greater and more desirable
to be found than Thou, O Jesus. Thou sayest to me:
I am the door. If anyone enters through Me,
he will be saved. If not, he must climb over like a robber.

Lord, in order fully to understand these divine words,
I should probably have to pray for many years.
Thou hast also said in Thy Gospel
of what Thou art the door.
Thou art the door of the Sheepfold and of the most holy
    Trinity,
of its infinite sanctity and beatitude.
Thou art the door to the love of the Three Persons.

Thou hast invited me to enter through Thee
into the joy of the Lord,
into the joy that the Father gives Himself
in knowing and in loving His Son,
into the joy that the Son receives from the knowledge

and the love of His Father.
Into the very joy which is none other than the Holy Spirit
since He is the love of the Father and the Son.

—Yes, My child, I am the door to this joy
because I am the door to love.
—But, Jesus, I know that if we observe Thy commandments,
we are called
to the beatific vision after death.
I believe it because the Church has taught me so.
But this recompense is for the other world.
In this world, I already possess a treasure, Thy friendship,
the union of my soul with Thine.
I am a member of Thy mystical body.

Now is not that the highest favor
we can dream of here below?

No, My child, I am all that, but I am also the door.
That is to say, I lead you to a higher gift.
A gift which, before you reach paradise,
your heavenly Father has already accorded you here below,
and which to Our very great displeasure
you ignore. For you seem to act
as if this gift were nothing to you.
You stop at the door and do not knock.

If you knocked, the Father would open to you and bid you
    enter
into the joy of the Lord.

I am the door to the life of the Trinity,
the life which is in Me and in the Trinity.
It overflows into you through the Holy Ghost.
The sap which is in the vine
flows also into the branches. You are My branch.
You are "one" with Me. But this unity
you compare to that of friendship and marriage.
And I—who alone understand it since I give it—
and who alone know that of the Father and of the Son
since I receive it from the Father—
I compare it only to that of the Father and the Son
in the indivisible Trinity.

It is the same unity—and not another—that I have asked of the
    Father,
in order that it may remain with Us,
as it remains between the Father and Me.
It is the unity that the Father has granted to My prayer,
that He has established forever in My mystical body
through the mission of the Holy Ghost.
It is the unity that I maintain and develop
every morning through the Holy Eucharist

and also through daily charity.
To this unity I am the door.
Hasten to enter through the door
and live not only on the side of commanded service
but in constant union with the Three Persons.

—What art Thou saying to me, O Jesus? This is the privilege
of the saints or of contemplative souls
whom the Holy Ghost raises to passive prayer,
highly favored disciples of Saint John of the Cross,
religious, most gifted for mystical contemplation.
As far as I am concerned, the door is closed.

That is precisely where you are wrong, My child,
Jesus says to me. Everybody is called, and you personally,
to enter into the banquet hall.
And there is no other way than through Me.
I will explain it to you further. But
first ask My Mother Mary for
the grace to open your mind and enlighten your faith.
I will show you how you are her son and My brother,
how you are a son of God.

XXXVIII. I Am the Door of the Sons of God

If you have prayed to My Mother Mary, Jesus says to me,
you will understand for what and of what I am the door.

I am the door not only to friendship with Jesus,
not only to the love which unites My Heart
with your poor, selfish heart,
but especially to the life of the three divine Persons.
I would not be a door were it not necessary for you
to pass beyond the threshold of the sacred dwelling
and beyond the simple friendship of sentiment and devotion.

That you, without dying of joy, might be able to live here
    below
the life of the three Persons
in an embrace whence They draw Their beatitude,
they have freely given you
the living water of sanctifying grace.

(174)

Having drunk of it from the sacramental chalice,
you possess a share in the divinity of Christ
which, without taking from you your human nature,
or your essential limitations, or your nothingness,
raises you up to a relation to the divine Persons
akin to that of the blood relationship of one family.
I am the door to this divine adoption
which is communicated to you in love.
Do not seek to see how this mystery is accomplished.
It is enough that you live with the three Persons
as an adopted son of God.
For the marvel of marvels,
the treasure hidden in the abyss of mercy,
the root of this sublime ennobling
is the Sonship I have made you share
through an unutterable communication
with the Word of God, with the Son of the Father.

I am the door to divine Sonship;
with Me, you are in reality a son of the Father.
I make you live with My life as a Son
in every possible way whereby I can render you able
of being truly, through Me, a son of God.

The Holy Ghost prepared Mary to be the Mother of God;
He prepared My humanity for the hypostatic union;

and He prepared you to become God's Son,
for the first two creations prepared the third.
I am the door to the sonship which is My privilege
in the Trinity. I give it to you that the Father,
adopting you, may love you as He loves Me,
with a Father's love.

But not only are you with Me
the object of My Father's love.
You are also with Me and through Me the principle
of the love of the Son for the Father.
The Father eternally receives from Me a love
identical to that which I receive from Him.
We are equal in love;
indeed, we are "one" in love.

But you, united to Me by the Holy Ghost and by charity,
love the Father with the same love as I,
and this love is "one" in Me with that of the Father.
It makes you "one" with Me and with My Father.

That would be impossible without Me.
No one comes to the Father except through Me.
There is no other filiation than Mine,
no other than that received from Me.
I am the door to that life of love.
How can you hesitate to pass through?

And, if you have gone through, how can you retrace your
   steps?

I will reveal to you something further
concerning the life of love which I give you.
This love which makes me "one" with the Father
is none other than the Holy Ghost.
For the sons of God, I am the door to the life of the Trinity.
If you are a son, you possess the Holy Ghost
and if you possess the Holy Ghost, you are a son of the Father.
And it is in the Holy Ghost that you love, that you pray,
that you offer sacrifice, that you praise, that you suffer,
that you work, that you live through charity.

Do you wish Me now, My dear child, My brother,
to unveil the sacrament of this mystery of love?
Look at My Heart: It is open,
it is the door to love,
it is the sign of the love of the Son for the Father.
It is not only the sign of that love; it possesses it in its fullness.
It has never loved with another love.
The Holy Ghost who fills it is My Spirit.
And it is from Him that all grace has sprung.
It is by Him that you receive the love of the Son for the Father.
You are a child of My pierced Heart.
Like My holy Mother Mary, keep all these truths in your soul,
and meditate on them, listening to her voice.

XXXIX.   I Am the Narrow Door

O Jesus, Thy mother has promised me
that if I want to live as a son of the Father
as a son of Thy Mother,
Thou wilt tell me the infallible secret
which will permit me to open the door and pass through
to enter into true divine life.
How can I fail to obey that maternal voice
which never deceives?

—If I say, My child, that this infallible secret
is in My Heart, you will readily believe Me,
and you will not hesitate to seek the charity of My Heart.
But if I tell you that this secret is in My *lifeless* Heart,
My Heart struck by the deadly lance,
dead to this temporal life and living only in God,
My Heart which beat no longer because it had no more blood,
My Heart pierced, My Heart wounded,
perhaps that will frighten you.

(178)

I remember My own fear in the garden.
My wounded Heart speaks to you: I am the narrow door.
You must pass through the Passion and through death.
Do you wish the door which is narrow? There is no other.
You have passed through it by receiving the sacraments.
In baptism, you died and you were buried
in My death and in My sepulcher.
You shared in My bloody sacrifice
through Mass and through Holy Communion.
You penetrated into the mystery of My Passion
by the sacrament of penance.
Everywhere the charity of My Heart has let you in
through the narrow door,
before giving you birth and growth in divine life.
You must pass through it every time that the Spirit
invites you to take a great step with Jesus Christ.

—What art Thou proposing to me, O Jesus? A life of sacrifice?
A life of immolation and of death?
A life in which my anguished love will perhaps be stifled,
no longer able to breathe for joy?

How blind you are, My child
and how little you trust Me.
But what has My Mother, Cause of your Joy, told you
if it is not a promise of greater joy?

Listen, then, to Me! A door is a doorway.

Narrow, it opens on infinite happiness;

as a field glass on a magnificent landscape,

it opens on the life of the Trinity.

If it is narrow, it is also not deep.

The threshold is a mere crack—one does not live on the
    threshold.

One lives either on one side or the other.

What is awaiting you this very day is the life of love,

that of the Son for the Father and in the Holy Ghost.

It is the life of Jesus risen;

it is the outpouring of the Holy Ghost through the living Christ

It is the outpouring, into the Church and into you

of the river of living water which will innundate you in such
    a way

that it will seem to flow from your soul as from a spring.

It is the union with the Father through filial love

in the profound joy of the spirit.

I am wrong in telling you that this life *awaits* you

for it is promised not only

at the end of your earthly life as you think.

It is given directly at baptism, at Holy Communion,

in the sacraments, in every act of love

(180)

in which you die to self by following Jesus Christ.
You must thus die in Christ
to enter the door to the life of the Trinity.
But each time that you die in Jesus
you rise again in Him; for Jesus is living and will never more
   die.
He is risen. Alleluia! Alleluia!
He rises again in you at every moment in which you die in Him.

His Heart in death is the sign of a love without reserve,
of a love which will make the son of man in you die.
But His Heart is also the Heart of the Son of God.
It is united hypostatically to the Word:
"I am the Resurrection and the Life," He said.
It is, then, the sign of an undying love which fills up
in you what is wanting to the Resurrection of Christ.
That is why My Heart says to you, "I am the narrow door
but the door to true divine life."

—O Jesus, what shall I render Thee for all the love which Thou
   dost manifest to me?
And what shall I render to Thy Mother Mary
for having cured the blindness of my spirit?
A light has dispelled the confusion of my mind.
I understand now the meaning of
those images which I used to love to employ:

"to enter into Thy Heart, to live in Thy Heart."
It is surely a question of living only of Thy love
and at the same time to die to all self-love,
to all that is not the filial love of Jesus for the Father,
to all love which is not received from the Heart of Jesus.
I understand now how the narrow door
of the Holy Trinity is Thy pierced Heart,
Thy Heart, that of the Son of God, living truly and forever.

XL. That You May Believe

Anguish is pressing my soul, the anguish of illusion.
Have I not been deceiving myself
in believing that as a son of God I share
in the love of the Word for the Father
in the most Holy Trinity?
O Jesus! O Mary, deliver me from the folly
of pride or of doubt.
Have I confused Jesus with the devil?
Have I believed too much or not enough?

My child, here is My Heart opened on the cross.
And here is My beloved disciple who bears testimony
to the outpouring of these last drops of blood and of water
which remained lifeless and divine in My Heart,
in My Heart drained by the excesses of love.
And John says he renders testimony "that you may believe."
For it is true that all the grace of Jesus
which makes you a son of God, a son of the Father,
and through which you can love God as He loves Himself,
is a reality known here below only by faith.

This grace is not sensible except—by a very rare favor—
in a flash of mystical illumination.
Normally you have life in God, of God, through God,
and you do not experience it with the senses any more than
   you experience God Himself.

It is a certain reality, but in faith.
You take hold of it, but in the obscurity of faith.
Nevertheless, when you die to the appearances of the flesh,
you immediately live entirely in the life of the Trinity
which is alone the source of all that is supernatural.
Your faith itself, my dearly beloved child,
is not what you think, a sort of taking of sides,
a blind wager to which you resolve yourself.
No, far from that. Your faith is a grace from the Heart of Jesus
and is already a real participation in the life of the Trinity.

Your faith, dim in your eyes, is in you a light from the Word.
It is a share—as much as you can take—
in the very knowledge that the Son has of the Father.
By faith you know the Father as He is known
by His Son in the eternal light,
because you have received the divine sonship.

You see, then, all the riches My Heart contains.
You believe because you adhere to the words and to the acts
which reveal to you the love of the Father.

(184)

You believe in the peerless testimony of My pierced Heart.
You love because My Heart has asked for your love.
But this faith and this love, gifts of My Heart,
are sensible signs of that loving intercourse
of the Father and of the Son in the Trinity
in which from this moment on, you have a share by your faith
    and love.
That is why My Heart says to you: I am the door.
And because faith and love exact the death
of our senses, of our mind and of our will,
My Heart says to you also: I am the narrow door.

—O Jesus, since, in union with Thee, I can know the Father;
since, in union with Thee, I can love the Father
according to the measure of the grace which every day
Thou dost lavishly bestow upon me,
shall I be foolish enough, blind enough, wretched enough,
to doubt for an instant that the tiniest act of courage
and of trust in Thy love returns me the hundredfold?
The hundredfold, I know, does not mean the same thing
a hundred times multiplied, but it is an absolute.
It is the happiness of the Father, of the Son, and of the Holy
    Ghost,
to which no created happiness can be compared,
which no suffering but Thine can purchase—
the suffering, O Jesus, of a God whose Heart was pierced by
    love.

XLI. Living Water

If you did know the gift of God,
Jesus said to me, seeing that I was thirsty,
more thirsty than the Samaritan woman,
you would perhaps ask Me for drink
and I would give you living water.

What is this living water to you, My child?
It is pure water, it is fresh water,
it is spring water which comes up clear
from remote depths—
it is water which quenches thirst and washes away stains.
Water which purifies, heels, and comforts. . . .

Saint Francis of Assisi called it his sister.
He saw it shooting out into space
like a ray of the sun
from the hands of the Creator.
And the immaculate Virgin caused it to well up
at Lourdes, from the fingers of a simple innocent girl;

no rottenness ever made it foul,

and it brought back health to the sick.

Living water was already flowing copiously in Paradise.

Adam and Eve knew no other;

it was their happiness.

In the midst of the desert, the people of Israel, dying of thirst,

drank plentifully of that miraculous water

which Moses had brought forth in abundance

when he struck the rock at God's command.

Living water in the hands of the Precursor,

served to baptize all the chosen race;

and the well-beloved Son, in whom the Father was pleased,

beheld it as a mirror

which reflected His divine holiness;

then, like His people and like all the sons of God, He was
    immersed in it.

But if you did know the gift of God,

you would know also that the living water is really only a
    symbol.

As a lamb recalls the Lamb of God,

as bread recalls the flesh of Christ in His sacrament,

all spring water, all pure and refreshing water,

is called "living water" because it recalls that sublime water

which the blow of the lance caused to stream forth with the
    blood,

from the divine Heart of Jesus on the cross.
Ah! Hold fast the knowledge that that is the only true living
    water;
for it is the only water which belongs to Jesus Christ Himself,
the only water which forms part of the humanity of the
    Incarnate Word,
as much as His blood, His members, and His life.

If you did know the gift of God
you would certainly ask Me to drink of that water
which comes from the Heart of Jesus.
The sweetness, the relish, the force,
the pure splendor of that water of Christ
is a sign of the grace which forms the beauty
of your soul, regenerated in baptism to the image of God.

If you are thirsty, come and drink.
It was to give the water of grace to poor men dying of thirst
that at the Feast of Tabernacles I cried out to the multitude
    in the Temple
with all the strength of that voice
of whose power Scripture speaks:
if anyone thirst, let him come to Me and drink!
He who believes in Me will drink
from a river of living water.

How is it that you do not ask Me
for that water, incomparable, celestial, divine,
which is served only at the table of the sons of God,
the drink of God Himself?
In order to quench the thirst of your soul,
is it necessary for me to reveal to you that that water, whose
source you know
is in the depth of My Heart,
is not only divine life
but also the symbol of the divine Person
whom Christ sends to you,
the Holy Ghost who proceeds from the Father and the Son
because He is Their mutual Love?

If you did know the gift of God
you would perhaps ask Me to drink
"that profusion of the Spirit" of which the water of My Heart
is the transparent and living image.
For the Spirit is the gift and the Bond of Love
as the water from My Heart is the sign of My exceeding-great
love.
It is My beloved disciple who in his Gospel bears witness to
you
of its eternal truth:
from his side will flow rivers of living water.

He said that of the Spirit who was to be received
by those who would believe in Him.

—O Jesus, how could I fail to believe in Thy immense mercy?
Thou wouldst give me an ocean of pure water,
Thou wouldst give me all the most delicate wines,
and all that creation holds, the most exquisite to the taste;
but if I have no thirst, if I have no desire to drink,
I would remain indifferent to all Thy wondrous offers.
But if I thirst, however slightly,
and so much the more if my thirst burns me like fire,
I would give all I have for a drop of living water.
Ah! When one has learned to know the living water,
is not the supreme grace to have thirst?
Is it not the urge to drink?

But while the pleasures of this world
violently excite my desire
alas! the infinite blessings which Thou offerest me
leave me unfeeling and without relish.
I hardly taste them now and then with the tip of my lips—
I prefer the waters of poisoned cisterns. . . .
Certainly I would like to be made thirsty,
like the saints, like the martyrs,
like so many contemplative souls,
like so many apostles more eager to despoil themselves
than other people are to be enriched. . . .

I see souls who seek suffering,
prayer, devotion, humiliation, the cross, thorns,
more than a miser money, more than a bridegroom his bride.
But as for me, I undergo them as unavoidable misfortunes.
I reject them every time I can.
Never have I experienced the slightest desire for them.
Ah! Lord, who will give me a thirst for the living water?
Thirst for the drink offered by Thy Heart,
thirst for Thy Holy Spirit?
Da mihi sitire fontem vitae.

—My child, I will excite in you the thirst which you beg,
if, with an ardent prayer and a sincere desire,
you approach the wound of My Heart.
But to approach My wound,
you must first mount Calvary.
Those who have fled the cities and have gone out to the desert,
those who have no more to live by but arid sand,
nakedness, solitude, and silence,
soon feel themselves burning with an unbearable thirst.
That is the secret of the thirst: voluntary poverty.
The desert is only an image of Calvary.
Calvary is the one true desert
where God has caused to spring forth the one fountain of life,
the only living water for eternal life,
from the Heart of Christ, struck by the soldier,
like the rock, struck by Moses.

Now, you have penetrated the mystery of the living water.
It is the divine life; it is the Holy Ghost.
But only that soul drinks it who has found the thirst
in the total abnegation of the desert,
and asks for drink from the pierced Heart of Jesus Christ.

XLII.   The Fire

The first word of Thy love
My God, was that of creation: *Fiat;*
and the first word of Thy creation
was that of light: *Fiat lux!*
Before there was light, shadows reigned
and the Spirit of God hovered over the waters.

The first word of the new creation
was the *Fiat* of Thy Mother Mary,
and from her womb came forth the light eternal
which enlightened the world into which the Word had come.
For the Word is the true light which enlightens
every man born of God, ready to receive Him.

When Thou didst render Thy last sigh,
shadows reigned again over the earth;
but the *Fiat* of the Resurrection
opened to us anew the eternal paradise

(193)

illumined by the light of the Lamb. . . .
And the new heavens and the new earth
will shine like diamonds in the sun.

If Thou art the light, O Jesus, Thy Spirit is the true Fire.
In the Bible, everywhere the divine presence is enveloped by
    fire.
Fire announces it, heralds it, veils it, adapts it to our vision.
Fire is the sanctity of God,
but it is also and especially Love.
For fire is the symbol of the Spirit,
because He is the Love of the Father and the Love of the Son.
Our Lord, speaking of His love,
said that He wished to enkindle the earth with His fire.
The Holy Ghost descended on the apostles in tongues of fire,
and the entire renovation of souls which they effected
was like a sudden conflagration enkindled by the fire of
    Pentecost.

That is why the Heart of Jesus is presented to us
as a furnace more ardent than all others;
a furnace whose flames are those of God Himself;
for Christ possesses the plenitude of the Spirit,
of His privileges, of His virtues, and of His gifts.
The Holy Spirit is His Spirit. He belongs to Christ,
he is Christ's as His very own.

The love which the Incarnate Word has for His Father
is the same as that of the Father for the Incarnate Word.

—You see, My child, Jesus says to me,
why I have inspired My Church and why I have asked from
    her
devotion to the Heart of her Spouse.
It is because My Heart is consumed by Fire,
the Fire which is the Spirit of God and His sanctity and His
    love.
No one has ever seen God except in Fire,
under the form of Fire, as a devouring Fire.
In showing My Heart pierced by love
again I have shown God in Fire.
Look upon My Heart and you will see God.
For God is pure Love. . . .
Offer My Heart enkindled by love
as Abel offered his first-fruits,
as the priests of Israel offered their holocausts in the Temple;
for I am the true Temple and the unique Holocaust.
Look upon the burning fire of My Heart and cast yourself
    into its flames.

For, My child, I desire you to be,
like Me and through Me,
enkindled by My Spirit, the fire of My love.

(195)

While there remains in you a spark of life
which is not penetrated by My flame,
you will not be like to Jesus,
nor fully risen wih Him.
I desire to give you with this fire, My sanctity and My love:
your sins will be consumed,
your flesh likewise;
your good deeds will pass through the flame,
purgatory will burn away all that the Spirit
has not yet transfigured in you.

Since I have given you My Spirit
His fire has been purifying you every day
through charity, through penance, and through the Eucharist.
But for all eternity He will make you live
in the glory and the light of My Resurrection.

That is why I have counseled you to have devotion to My
    Heart.
It reminds you that the religion of the Father, of the Son, and
    of the Holy Ghost
is a religion of love,
that without the spirit of love God would not exist,
God would not have called any creature to His own happiness,
Christ would not have taken your flesh
nor would He have died for you. . . .

Pray, then, for this Fire, with cries and tears if you can.
Pray to the Father and to the Son for Their Spirit;
make your prayer through My Heart, through its wound,
by the water and the blood of My wounds,
by My entire Passion:
the Father will give Him to you
and I will give Him to you.
Then, with your heart burning with the same fire as Mine,
you will love God as He loves Himself;
you will love men as God Himself loves them;
you will want to inflame the earth with love for Jesus Christ.
And what anguish will press your soul
as long as the holocaust of Christ in His mystical body
is not yet consummated to the glory of His Father!

Oh! Come, Holy Spirit, fill the hearts of Thy faithful
and enkindle in them the fire of Thy love!

XLIII.   The Blood of Christ

My child, I would like to talk to you about My blood,
about the blood which I received from My immaculate
    Mother;
about the blood which in my love I shed to the last drop
to redeem all sinners;
about the blood which millions of priests of every race,
ever since the time of My apostles in the Cenacle,
have drunk and do still drink from their chalices,
even to the consummation of the world;
about the blood which Saint John saw flowing in Jerusalem
at the wedding feast of the Lamb:
those who wore white robes
came out of the great affliction
and washed and whitened their robes
in the blood of the Lamb.

My Heart is priestly through the action of the Holy Ghost,
but it is so also by the outpouring of its blood.

For I am Christ, the priest, who offered His own blood,
having poured it out into the cup of the new covenant
to seal the eternal pact of adequate reparation,
and the definitive union of creatures with God.
Then it was shed under the impulse of love
on the ground of the agony, on all the way to Calvary.
I took the blood of man only to pour it out
in testimony of My love.

That blood which was poured out is that of the sovereign
    Priest; He alone has penetrated
into the tabernacle made not by the hand of man.
The earth has drunk and will drink all the blood of humanity,
but that of the Incarnate Word has been carried into the
    sanctuary;
not a drop will be lost.

The apostles did not suspect that future Resurrection,
when they saw that blood in the agony, reddening the
    ground. . . .
The executioners had not the least idea of it,
when their whips and their lances
and their sharp nails caused it to bespatter
their dirty hands and their filthy garments. . . .
Not one believed that the blood of God
was blood which would remain eternally living and all-saving.

And you, My child, on whom I have bestowed the faith,
what are you doing with My precious blood?
You know that I poured it out for you,
not through weakness, but of My own free will, as a willing
    martyr,
through the force of a love which wants to surrender itself
    entirely. . . .
You know that it belongs to you, like all My human nature,
like My Heart, like My life.

You know that, if My mystical members live in Me,
they live mystically of My blood
present in the chalice of the holy sacrifice
and present also in the host which they receive in Communion.
You know that if a sacrament purifies your soul
it can happen only through the shedding of My blood. . . .
My redeeming blood is always there,
in all the supernatural life of the Church. . . .
for without the outpouring of My blood, there is no redemption.

But what are you doing with My precious blood?
You can offer it to My Father, if you will and when you will,
not only for your sins but for the sins of all mankind,
and also to obtain every grace;
for graces are bought not at the price of gold—
gold has no more value than dirt in the purchasing of
    graces. . . .

But only at the price of the blood of God, shed through love.
There is no grace more precious than My blood.

Then the strangest thing, the most incomprehensible,
the most unreasonable, the most humiliating,
that which most shows the folly of man
is his lack of confidence in the blood of God,
even when he is in the state of greatest despair.
It is like seeing a millionaire
wondering if he can purchase his daily bread.

What are you doing with My precious blood?
Poor child, for whom the holy Mass holds no interest,
who does not know how to follow it,
nor what the priest is doing—his back turned—
and with a server who is bustling around the altar and who
    rings a bell.
When you offer My body and My blood
with the Church, with the whole priesthood, with the
    officiating priest,
you can glorify God, thank Him, make reparation for sin,
save the dying, deliver the souls in purgatory,
give to your most ardent desires for the kingdom of God
an almost infallible power of intercession. . . .

But you seem to be ignorant of the power of My blood,
of the gift which I have made of it to all baptized souls.

Otherwise you would spend your time
in putting to use, for the greatest good of souls,
the unfathomable riches of the priestly Heart of Jesus.

If all souls prayed with My blood,
not a single one would be damned.
With My blood, all men should enter heaven.
No one goes to hell, except, of his own free will,
he crosses the frontier of My blood which has been shed in
        torrents.
It is this insane contempt which results in
the folly and the remorse of the damned.

—But, O Jesus, where shall I find Thy blood
so that my confidence may no longer spin and turn dizzily?
For everything seems to me to be changing, fleeting, elusive.

—My blood is in My glorified body,
in the priestly Heart of Christ, eternal priest and victim.
—But Lord, how can we here below
be washed, purified, santified, sated, inebriated,
with the blood of Thy risen body?

My child, it is through the power of the Holy Ghost.
For, if My Heart has shed all its blood,
it is because It has learned from My Father

(202)

that by this effusion, It would fill the whole universe with His
   Spirit.
My blood was a true gift, not so much of itself
as because of the Spirit of love
whose extension over mankind it merited
and of which it was the symbol.
That is why My apostle Paul
attributes all the blessings of the Redemption
to the blood of Christ and to the Spirit without distinction.

More and more, then, My beloved son, you see
that My Heart is that of a priest
and that devotion to My Heart
is also devotion to the Holy Spirit.
The Spirit is Love. That divine love
has been overflowing on this world like a torrent
ever since the day of Pentecost,
because Christ had shed all His blood
even to the last drops which fell from His Heart as it was
   pierced.

Such is the profound significance of this devotion
that it comprises a great many others:
to the Holy Ghost, to the Passion, to the cross,
to the precious blood, to the holy sacrifice of the Mass,
to the priesthood, to the apostolate.

All the mysteries
of the charity of the Father and the Son
converge toward the Heart of Jesus pierced on the cross.

Come, creating Spirit:
with Thy light scatter the darkness from my mind.
Make me understand to what purpose Jesus has shown me
His pierced Heart and has spoken of His despised love.
Pour into my heart the abundance of Thy love.

XLIV.   We Will Establish Our Dwelling in Him

Let me tell you of the greatest gift of My love.

Men can give you nothing except what is human.
But I can communicate to you what properly belongs to God,
what no creature of himself can see, attain, or conceive.
He receives it, lives in it, enjoys it as if he were God.
He shares in those goods and perfections through which God
    is God
without being God himself.
He possesses them in the obscurity of faith
awaiting the full clarity of vision.

I am Jesus, that absolutely unique man
who gives not only created gifts but above all the uncreated
    Gift.
I do not give things, even divine things, so to speak,
but solely living Persons.

I am that man absolutely unparalleled
who gives to you the Father, the Son, and the Holy Ghost,
the three Persons of the blessed Trinity,
so that you live of Their life.
You are of the family of God
sharing His glory and His happiness.
I am that man absolutely unparalleled
who gives you the eternal Father, the all-powerful Father,
the Father incomprehensible in His greatness,
because He is the necessary source of everything.
I give Him to you in the only possible way,
through sonship, through My own sonship,
which is like no other
because it does not in any way separate Me from My Father.
You are so perfectly His son with Me
that if I am begotten by the Father,
so are you, receiving His own life;
and if I am eternally in His bosom,
so too are you, through generation by grace
for all eternity.

I give you the Son by incarnation,
but if you are not the flesh of the Son
you nevertheless have communion
in the flesh and the blood of the Son.
I have given you and do give you daily, according to your
    pleasure,

My flesh and My blood sacramentally.
This gift, inseparable from My person
and from My divinity, and from all that belongs to Me
makes you fully a living member of the Son,
a new creature, born of God.

I am that man absolutely unparalleled
who gives you the Holy Spirit;
do not let the word "spirit" deceive you into thinking
that I am nothing but a scholar or a thinker.
The Spirit is also a divine Person.
I give you the Third Person of the True God
so faithfully, so completely, so really,
that all that man possesses by nature
is only an image of what he possesses through the Spirit.

I am that absolutely unique man
who gives these three Persons and all that He has, freely.
In exchange for these infinite bounties, He asks nothing.
The poorest, provided that he has a little love,
not even pure love, but simply a longing,
the desire, like that of a begger who stretches out his hand;
be he sinner, be he criminal,
if he regrets his folly and aspires to true life,
I do not hesitate an instant to give to him
the holy Trinity which will dwell in his unworthy soul
day and night as a prisoner of his faith and of his love.

Try now to see the abyss of that love.

There exists no other like it.

He who gives, has had to die to give.

To glorify the love of the Father, of the Son, and of the Holy Ghost,

he had to bear testimony by the Passion,

through martyrdom, through a fathomless abasement of Himself.

Your gratuituous sharing in the life of the Trinity

was so extraordinary and so incomparably sublime

that to pay for it at the price of the blood and of the humiliation of God

was not to purchase it too dear.

I am that man unparalleled who has paid for all the rights

of your filiation, of your purification, of your participation in the divine life.

Ah! why do so few men know Me,

so few listen to Me, so few follow Me, so few receive Me?

And you, how do you listen to Me and how do you receive Me?

One day, repeating what I said on the cross, "I thirst,"

I uttered this agonized cry:

"behold this Heart which has loved men so much,

even to exhausting and consuming itself to show His love for them.

And in return, what do I receive for the most part?

Nothing but indifference and ingratitude
especially coldness and irreverence
in the sacrament of My love."
Only eternity and the light of glory will make you understand
the depth of the love of this Heart.

But here below can you not show yourself
less insensible and less ungrateful?
Ask this grace of My Mother Mary
who alone has truly understood the love of My Heart.

XLV. Receive the Holy Spirit

My God, Thou couldst have given me the whole universe
and all that it contains and all that it produces
and all its dominion and all its pleasures,
all the gifts of body, of heart, and of intellect.
If Thou hadst not communicated to me Thy Holy Spirit,
without question I would have been weighed down with Thy
    benefits,
beyond my desert and beyond all measure,
but I would be infinitely less rich than I am.

With all that wealth, I could be damned.
What would it profit me to gain the whole world if I were
    going to lose my soul?
What is absolutely necessary to me is charity.
Saint Paul said that if I had not charity,
I would be *nothing*. Everything else would avail me nothing,
for material treasures are vain. He does not even mention them.
And vain are the most exalted gifts of the spirit,

even that of the fullness of faith,
of a faith that could move mountains.
If I had not charity, I would be nothing, affirms the apostle.
Nothing, even if I were a great benefactor of humanity,
even if I delivered my body to be burned,
wonder-worker, scholar, creator, magician,
nothing matters; I would be nothing without charity.

Nothing, in fact, before God, in the eyes of God,
nothing in death, the tomb, corruption.
Hardly a remembrance, a shade among shades,
nothing in eternity, in the judgment of God,
for the Life, the Truth, the Way
is not the creature, but the Incarnate Word.
Yet it is necessary that this Word love us
and that He unite us to Himself by charity.

—But, My child, Jesus says to me, if you are nothing without
    charity,
with charity alone, you do not have
all your greatness, all your wealth, all your power,
all your happiness, and all the perfection of your being,
for your true worth comes from the Holy Ghost whom I have
    given you with charity.
He is your Spirit without ceasing to be My Spirit.
Receive the Holy Ghost, My Spirit, My Love.

If—by an impossibility—you possessed charity without the Holy
    Ghost
this virtue would not give God to you.
Our intimacy, however close, would then be
infinitely inferior to what it is in reality.

For infused charity is a *thing*, it is not God.
I, the Son, am not one God with a *thing*.
The Holy Spirit whom you possess is God.
And I am one God with the Holy Spirit.
Our closeness, then, through the Spirit is infinitely profound.
To give you the Spirit is to give you God
and to give you God is to give you at the same time the Son
    and the Father.
Therefore you possess God by grace with the Holy Spirit.
He alone makes you capable of living of the life of God.
You possess not only supernatural life
but also its fruitful and inexhaustible source.

Sources here on earth need to be fed.
They receive what they give.
You also are a source which receives all that it gives.
If it gives supernatural life, it has received it.
If it gives natural life, it has received it.
Necessarily, you are nothing of yourself,
but the Holy Spirit in you is not a created force.

(212)

Proceeding from the Father and the Son, He is equal to the
    Father and to the Son.
He is source as is the Father, He is source as is the Son.
He alone has the privilege of proceeding from the Father and
    the Son,
of being the Gift of the Father and of the Son, without ceasing
    to be God.

Now perhaps you will understand a little less imperfectly
how extraordinary is the gift of My Heart, the Holy Spirit,
the Holy Spirit, who is the Spirit of the Father and the Spirit
    of the Son.
By His outpouring of love, you are included
in the ineffable exchange of the Son's love for the Father
and of the Father's love for the Son.
Both are united by the spiration of the Spirit.
By the spiration that you receive,
you love the Father as the Son Himself loves Him.
Receiving the Spirit of Their mutual love
through the same Spirit you restore to Them what They have
    given you;
a sort of equality is established between you and God
on the ground of love, on the ground of gratitude.

O admirable interchange! O prodigy of love!
It is not especially in considering the chastisements of God

but in considering His love that you must proclaim with Saint
    Paul:
O inexhaustible depth of the wisdom
and of the knowledge of God.
How incomprehensible are His designs
how inscrutable His ways.
Who has ever known the mind of the Lord?
Yes, of Him, through Him, for Him
are all things. To Him be glory forever. Amen.

But here, My child, is a new and supreme tenderness
of which too many ungrateful souls never dream.
Possessing with Me, in Me, and through Me
the same indivisible Spirit, the same breath of life,
the same spiration of love,
you possess, by this same communication,
a single heart, the Heart of the living Jesus,
the Heart, sorrowful, wounded, and risen.
In becoming incarnate, I was sure
that, under the human form of a heart like your own,
you would better understand the gift of My Spirit.
What have I not devised in order that I might be understood
    by men?
You know the nature, the longings, the torments, the follies,
the thousand kinds of joy and sorrow
of human love.

In that way you fathom a part of the love
of the Son of God who was made man and who speaks to you.
The infinite difference which distinguishes us, without
   separating us,
is that your love is poor, weak, and blind,
and mine is that of God, united to yours without any possible weakness or shortcoming.
There is no law to limit the continuous flowing
of the Holy Spirit who is the divine Spirit of God, to the human
   soul,
of the uncreated Love to created.

Now here is where you will recognize the tenderness of which
   I was speaking.
If you possess the Spirit, you possess the love of My Heart,
you possess the life of My Heart, you possess My Heart.
For if I willed to have a human heart
it was to make you appreciate better
the value and the meaning of the gift of My Spirit,
His presence in Me as in you,
His life in Me as in you,
the strength of His impetus
in you as in Me,
and all that He could do in you
if, like Me, you abandon yourself to His control.
You believe you understand the Holy Ghost,

(215)

but if I had not revealed to you the life of My Heart,

you would know nothing of Him except that He is God

and that He is a mystery more obscure than the Father and
the Son;

and knowing almost nothing of the magnificent gift of My
Heart

you would know almost nothing of Him;

you would be ignorant of the grandeur and the power

of the love which you can have for God.

Do you see now why I have revealed My Heart to you,

dear child whom I call to love!

—O Heart of Jesus, who hast given me Thy Spirit

and who livest in me by Thy Spirit,

fill my heart with Thy love,

enkindle in it that fire which consumes *Thee*

and grant that there be in me no will,

no desire, no attachment, no pleasure

other than those which Thou makest me share with Thee

through the Holy Ghost.

XLVI.   That You May Be One with the Father and the Son

When, during prayer, I speak to you of My Heart,
it is more often of My Holy Spirit that we converse,
Jesus tells me. For one cannot imagine a gift of love
either in God, or in man, greater than the Holy Ghost.
The mystery of the Trinity is consummated in the Spirit.
Likewise, the mystery of the virginal conception of the Son
    of God,
likewise, the mystery of the priesthood of Christ,
likewise, every mystery of Jesus up to the Resurrection—
the Ascension, Pentecost, and the whole life of the mystical
    body
are the work of the Holy Ghost, the Third Person of the
    blessed Trinity.
That is the reason why the Heart of Christ
is at the center of all Christianity.

We are told that the Holy Ghost is the soul of the mystical
    body.

(217)

As your soul assembles all your members into one union
and as your heart distributes life through the blood,
so My Heart which has given you the Spirit
unites by the Spirit the numberless parts
of the mystical body and animates them with a divine life.
That is why the Spirit has chosen as symbols
realities without form, without figure and without number,
which out of many things, form only one.
Thus water, which covers and envelops things most perfectly,
fire which turns everything into the devouring flame,
wind which knows no barriers,
light more subtle and more penetrating than water,
blood in which all the cells are bathed and are vivified,
the dove which flew over the deluge in which all hatreds
        perished
and announced peace to men,
the rainbow which is the sign of the eternal covenant.
Is there any creature whose function is reunion?
It is a symbol of the Holy Ghost.

But this unity is not only a fact;
it is also a power of action
infinitely superior to the universal pull of gravitation.
This power in all souls urged on by charity
is the same, indivisible. In all the saints without exception,
even in Christ and His Mother, it is the same,
because it is the Holy Ghost.

Thus when the Holy Ghost gives you love,
and you love your neighbor through charity,
who then is it who loves? Assuredly you,
but assuredly it is also Jesus,
for your Spirit is His Spirit.
And when you love your neighbor, through a mystical harmony,
   it is also
the Virgin Mary who loves your neighbor,
it is the saints, it is pure souls
who love your neighbor with you,
for My Spirit is their Spirit.

Charity has the same source in all.
Love, common to all, makes the Communion of Saints.
The Communion of Saints is an article of faith.
Nothing is more certain than an article of faith.

If then you pray with the Holy Ghost,
there is in the entire Communion of Saints but one prayer:
that of Jesus and of His members.
And if you suffer, there is only one suffering:
that of Jesus and of His members.
And if you merit, there is only one merit:
that of Jesus and of His members,
because there is only one Spirit:
that of Jesus and of His members.
And that is why all your supernatural acts profit

(219)

with Mine to the life of the entire body.

And the acts of other members profit you

in your wretchedness, you who, in your poverty, are nothing
apart from the whole.

The branch produces the grape through the vine

and the vine through the branch.

Both are sterile

if they are not in each other.

If you wish, My child, to live in truth,

do not isolate yourself, do not separate yourself, do not with-
draw into yourself

for any purpose, whether it be for prayer, for suffering, for
meriting,

or for praising God in joyfulness.

But always remember that, living in one Spirit,

you live in one body with all men,

with all saints and all sinners,

with Jesus, the Head of the whole body.

Jesus bears with Him the sins of the body; bear them with
Him.

Jesus prays for all the members; pray for all with Him.

Jesus suffers in all His members; suffer for all with Him.

Jesus works in all His members; work for all with Him.

If you are alone, unite yourself with all invisibly.

If you are with others, unite yourself with all visibly.

There is no Christian who cannot do this marvelous thing:
act at once as an individual and as a member.
He is never alone if he so desires, never abandoned,
because My Spirit is at the same time in him and in everyone.
Never has human word equaled those words which have ex-
pressed My love:
behold this Heart which has loved men so much
that it has asked the Father that all may be "one"
as the Father and the Son are "one."
Behold this Heart which has been fully heard
because it prayed with the love of the Son.

A NOTE ON THE TYPE

IN WHICH THIS BOOK WAS SET

This book is set in Caledonia, a Linotype face created in 1939 by W. A. Dwiggins, which is by far one of the best book types created in the last 50 years. It has a simple, hard-working, feet-on-the-ground quality and can be classed as a modern type face with excellent color and good readability. The designer claims Caledonia was created by putting a little of each of Scotch Roman, Bulmer, Baskerville and Bodoni together and producing a lively crisp-like book type. This book was composed and printed by the Wickersham Printing Company, of Lancaster, Pa., and bound by Moore and Company of Baltimore. The typography and design of this book are by Howard N. King.